FISHING'S
STRANGEST®
TALES

Other titles in the STRANGEST series

Titles coming soon

FISHING'S STRANGEST TALES

Extraordinary but true stories
from over 200 years of angling history

TOM QUINN

PORTICO

ACKNOWLEDGEMENTS

For help with research, flute playing, sleeping, badminton and the loan of
rare books and magazines thanks are due to: the Hon. Emma Westall, Richard
Green, David Gadnos, John Marston, the staff at the British Library and all the
poor souls whose long-forgotten books I have plundered. I'd also like to thank
Jane Donovan at Portico Books and Sarah Barlow for turning a sow's ear into
a silk purse.

First published in the United Kingdom in 2017 by
Portico
1 Gower Street
London
WC1E 6HD

An imprint of Pavilion Books Company Ltd

ISBN 978-1-91104-245-7

A CIP catalogue record for this book is available from the British Library.

10 9 8 7 6 5 4 3 2 1

Reproduction by Mission Productions Ltd, Hong Kong
Printed and bound by Bookwell, Finland

This book can be ordered direct from the publisher at www.pavilionbooks.com

CONTENTS

GHOULISH BAIT

ENGLAND, 1800

At the end of the eighteenth century many of London's rivers were still bright, sparkling and clean. Though the River Fleet had long been smothered by bricks and mortar, the Wandle in Wandsworth was still one of the best trout rivers in the South East, while the River Lee a little north of where it joined the Thames in what is now the East End was a wonderful mixed fishery. Chub, dace, roach, bream, barbel and trout thrived in the river and London fishermen walked in their droves on a Sunday morning to fish it.

On this particular Sunday morning two young city clerks reached the river from their lodgings in Holborn in a little over two hours. They began fishing, but after three hours not a single fish had touched either of their baits, so they left their rods and wandered along the banks in search of other, perhaps more successful, anglers. Half a mile (800m) away they came across a man who seemed too old even to be alive let alone be fishing. He had a long hazel rod with no reel, but all around him on the bank lay barbel, bream and trout. Despite appearances this old man clearly knew what he was doing – or he was just remarkably lucky.

The two unsuccessful fishermen began to talk to him and it quickly became clear that the one thing he enjoyed as much if not more than fishing was talking – more specifically talking about fishing. He had fished every

Sunday on this particular stretch of the Lee for 40 years and knew every bend and eddy as well as he knew the inside of his own house. He told them about his childhood on a remote Hertfordshire farm and about how he had walked to London every now and then driving geese all the way to be sold in the London markets. He told them about his knowledge of the weather and of the moods of the fish, but somehow he never mentioned the bait he used. They tried hints at first and then direct questions, but he simply smiled and changed the subject. At last the two anglers grew desperate and they told the old man that they would pay him a golden sovereign if he would only tell them what he used as bait. The prospect of gold did the trick and he showed them the great fatty lumps that he kept in his baitbox. What on earth was this strange, faintly disgusting bait?

'It's manfat,' said the old man with a sinister grin. 'Every few weeks I go down to Newgate and ask to speak to the surgeons. They're very helpful. When they've cut down the hanged they dissect them or bury them in lime, but if you know who to ask and how to ask you can always get plenty of the fat the surgeons scrape from inside the skin of the dead. The dead don't need it any more. The doctors have no use for it, so why shouldn't God's little fishes – and those who pursue them – have the benefit of it? And by God it works a treat – there's nothing like it. When you get some – it costs a penny a pound – you take my advice. Leave it a week in a cool place till it begins to turn. Pound and mash it every day until you have a fine and slightly sticky paste. Nothing beats it for fishing the Lee. But do you know there's one thing even better than man's fat for fishing? See if you can guess what it is?'

The two men exchanged glances and then confessed they had no idea.

'Woman's fat!' came the answer. It's harder to get of course because not so many are hanged and when they are why there's a rush for Newgate by all the roach fishers from Islington to Cheapside.'

The two men thanked the old man and told him it was time they returned to their rods. As they walked off they heard him shout.

'I haven't tried the fat of a child yet, but that I should think would be best of all!'

SHOEMAKER'S RECORD
SCOTLAND, 1810

Wealthy fishermen with the very best tackle money can buy don't inevitably catch the most fish, nor even the biggest individual specimens. Skill is a great deal more than half the battle and luck is always lurking ready to upset the arrogant claims of the so-called expert. This is part of the great appeal of fishing.

A case in point was the shoemaker of Aberlour whose success in landing one of the biggest salmon ever caught in Scotland – and with the most rudimentary tackle – was still being celebrated long after the shoemaker himself had gone to meet his maker.

Duncan Grant was a good shoemaker but he neglected his job for the river. He was obsessed with fishing despite having a heavy, clumsy old reel and a rod that had already seen better days when he bought it 30 years earlier. But Duncan was a determined man. He also knew the river better than any other man living and he had a sixth sense about where the fish would lie whatever the conditions.

One day he was fishing the Elchies Water a little way north of Aberlour. He tried one or two pools without success before arriving at a very deep, rapid pool called the Mountebank.

He threw his line out, down and across the water and no sooner had it begun to settle than a long, steady menacing pull told him a fish had taken. He lifted his rod and an almighty battle began.

Duncan's cast – the short length of fine line nearest the hook – was made from some 30 pieces of horsehair woven into one thick strand. By the standards of the early nineteenth century this was strong tackle indeed, but it had little effect on the fish, which moved steadily up and down the pool, but always staying deep.

Seven hours later the light had failed and Duncan still hung on, but he was exhausted and on the verge of deciding to cut his line and accept defeat. Then he had an idea that would allow him to rest, but also give him warning if the fish – sulking at the head of the pool under a huge boulder – made a dash for it.

He lay on the bank on top of the butt of his rod, pulled off several loops of line from his reel and threaded them ingeniously through his teeth.

After a sleep of nearly three hours the shoemaker was woken by a savage pull on his head. In a second he leapt to his feet with his rod well up, aware that the fish had left the sanctuary of the boulder and was heading rapidly down the pool.

Exactly 12 hours after he'd hooked the fish the shoemaker – alone and unaided – landed a 55lb (25kg) salmon.

RAT RUN

ENGLAND, 1816

The vicar of Salisbury in 1816 was one Josiah Carter. He was an enthusiastic fly fisherman in the days when live flies were still used and fly casting – in the modern sense – had yet to be invented. The Georgian technique, if it can be called that, was to use a very long rod, perhaps as much as 18ft (5.5m), and allow the wind to carry your long horsehair line, with daddy-long-legs or whatever attached to your hook, out to the middle of the stream.

Whipping rods and silk lines heavy enough to be cast back and forth were in their infancy and most fly fishermen, like the vicar, simply collected a tinful of real insects and proceeded to dibble them across the surface of the water. Of course in the early nineteenth century the pressures of pollution and over-fishing were unknown in most areas and large stocks of unsophisticated trout made game fishing that much easier, which is why our intrepid vicar often came back with a basketful of fish.

But on this particular day the trout were unresponsive. The vicar and several of his friends had enjoyed several good days on other stretches, but the weather, on this day, had turned against them. Loath to give up, the vicar fished on. Two hours later his fly landed on the water for the umpteenth time, there was a huge boil at the surface and a giant rat took the fly. It fought – as the vicar explained later on – like a tiger before he was able to bring it to the net.

Most of the vicar's friends assumed that, having landed the rat, he simply released it or knocked it on the head. So they were astonished six months later to visit the vicar and find, in a glass case in pride of place above his fireplace, a very large rat beautifully stuffed by one of the top London taxidermists.

The vicar had even asked the taxidermist to attach the hook and the final 6in (15.2cm) of line that had landed his great prize. And at dinner parties from that day forth he always boasted that any fool could catch a trout; 'only a very skilful angler could catch a rat the size of that one!'

BIRD OF PREY

ENGLAND, 1821

Before the disgraceful use of toxic chemicals on the land in the 1960s, Britain was a wildlife-rich place. This had its downside as many elderly people still recall. In summer flies and biting insects were, for example, far more numerous than they are now, but there were good things too – far more songbirds, otters, hares and badgers, for example. Best of all, in the nineteenth century there were no motorcars spewing fumes all over the place and a less densely populated countryside meant birds of prey, even eagles, were still common in many areas, which may explain the following story.

  A Mr Roberts from Carlisle was fishing the River Eden in Cumbria when he hooked a trout. Now most of the Eden's trout at this time weighed just a few ounces and there were so many of them that it was difficult to get through to anything bigger. Most fishermen were therefore happy to accept that a big bag of little fish was the most they could expect. However, as soon as he hooked this particular fish, Mr Roberts knew that he'd achieved the impossible. He'd hooked a big trout and from the feel of the thing it probably weighed nearer 2lb (0.9kg) than one. Terrified that it might get off he played it with the utmost care. He led it gently up and down the river and silently prayed each time it leapt and somersaulted in its efforts to get free. But at last it began to tire and he drew it across the water to the waiting net.

At that precise moment a massive bird of prey – Mr Roberts later claimed it must have been an osprey or an eagle – swooped down and along the river, talons dragging viciously below it. The bird hit the fish at about 30mph (48.3km/h) and scooped it into the air to the utter astonishment of Mr Roberts. The eagle – if that was what it was – soared into the sky. Mr Roberts's best ever trout from the Eden dangled beneath it. Mr Roberts, normally a sober, churchgoing man, let out a series of terrible oaths. Line was shooting away off his reel as the bird steered a course towards the distant hills. Mr Roberts took up the slack line, but the instant the bird found itself being tugged in the wrong direction, it let go of the trout. The fish fell into the middle of the river, but when Mr Roberts reeled in, he found that the best trout he'd ever hooked in the Eden was just a mangled wreck.

DEAD-SHEEP BAIT
ENGLAND, 1823

Anyone who reads Mrs Beeton's famous cookbook will know that our ancestors did not do things by halves. Mrs Beeton's recipes – 'take six pounds of butter for the sauce' reads one recipe – are clearly designed to feed families of no fewer than 15. Doing things on the grand scale was once an everyday part of fishing too, but few reached the level achieved by one aristocratic barbel fisher who had a house on the Thames just outside London.

In the early nineteenth century game fishing had not been tarnished by the rather snooty image it earned for itself during the early part of the twentieth. Pike fishing in many places was more sought after than salmon and trout fishing and men were as keen to catch chub and carp as to catch anything else.

Barbel, on the grounds that they are very hard-fighting fish – were much prized, though not for the table as they are virtually inedible. Our aristocratic fisherman liked fishing for barbel because they were easily the biggest fish in his part of the river and when the fancy took him he could simply walk to the end of his lawn to start to fish. However, he did not like to leave things to chance and therefore spent at least a week or two preparing for each barbel fishing outing. He would start by telling one of his keepers to hang a whole dead sheep from the bough of a tree that overhung the river. Each day he would inspect the carcass to make sure it was alive with maggots. Day and night a stream of maggots fell from the dead sheep into the river. The fish – of every species – would have been queuing up to eat them.

After a week or ten days the fisherman would send his men on a worm-hunting expedition. They would scour the lawns night after night collecting the biggest juiciest lobworms they could find. When almost a barrelful had been collected they were taken down to the water's edge by his servants, placed in a boat and rowed out to a position just upstream of the dead sheep in the tree. Here they were tipped into the water. On the morning this happened the fisherman would make sure he was ready at the water's edge, rod in hand, within an hour of the worms being thrown in. He used the latest London tackle – a long hazel rod and silk line on a winder. Six worms would be attached to his hook by his keeper and swung out into the river. If he didn't quickly hook a good fish the servants knew he would be in a rage, but of course after such meticulous preparation he almost always caught a fish every cast.

On the day he caught a record number of barbel – over 60 according to one account – he had offloaded a wagonload of worms into the stream. From the first cast that June morning he knew that every barbel for miles around had congregated in that short stretch of water in front of his house.

But though he caught fish after fish he didn't land a single specimen. And the reason – no sooner had he hooked a fish than he passed his rod to one or other of his gillies, for this was a time when all the skill of fishing was believed to lie in the hooking. The brute force business of playing and landing the fish was something for the lower orders.

All that long day barbel after barbel was hauled to the bank. Each fish was hooked by the landowner and played by one of his keepers. At the end of the day the wagon that had brought the worms to the water was virtually filled with fish. They were carried off and fed to the local pack of foxhounds. Among the enormous bag there were said to have been several individual fish of 16–17lb (7.3–7.7kg). Just one fish that size today would cause a sensation in the fishing world, but our Georgian aristocrat, having grown bored of the sport by mid-afternoon, went back to his house, fell asleep and forgot all about it.

VICAR'S LUCK

SCOTLAND, 1838

Salmon are mysterious creatures. We still don't know quite how they find their way back from the sea to the rivers where they were born and it was only in the 1960s that scientists discovered where most Atlantic salmon go to feed. To many, of course, that particular scientific discovery was a disaster because it meant that salmon, which in world terms had never been a particularly successful species, were netted ruthlessly. Anglers, naturally, wanted fewer fish netted on the high seas so that more would end up in the rivers, but few would deny that the angler's impact on total numbers of salmon would always be negligible.

When they reach their home rivers, salmon still behave in a way that baffles the scientists. We have no real idea why they take a fly, a spinner or bait. They don't eat in fresh water so why do they do it? The most likely explanation is that baits and spinners either remind them of creatures they ate while in the sea or irritate them and arouse an aggressive attacking instinct. But whatever the reason the mystery is part of the appeal for the angler. And even the most experienced salmon anglers have strange days with this strangest of all game fish. One of the oddest ever recorded involved two salmon in a series of remarkable coincidences and all in the space of one day.

An elderly vicar was staying with friends whose house was just a few hundred yards from the mighty River Tweed.

The vicar was a keen angler and every day of his two-week stay he fished for at least a few hours. On his last day he was fishing with a massive and very heavy 20ft (6.1m) greenheart rod. He hooked a very big salmon that rocketed from one end of the pool to the other before leaping into the air in a series of quite unstoppable cartwheels. The vicar held his breath and dropped the point of the rod while all this was going on. This was without question the biggest salmon he'd ever hooked and he was determined to land it. Twenty minutes into the battle the fish was cruising gently up and down near the far bank but right at the surface of the water. His great dorsal fin could easily be made out. The vicar, convinced that his fish was tiring, exerted a little more pressure; the fish's head came out of the water and at that very moment, with a huge crack, the top 4ft (1.2m) section of the rod broke off, slid down the line and hit the fish right in the head. Despite the break in the rod the fish came in to the net as meekly as a lamb, clearly stunned by the blow from the rod top. An hour later, with a 20-pounder (9.1kg) on the bank, the vicar was back in action with his spare rod. On his third cast he hooked another good fish. He confidently expected another ferocious battle. Instead he watched in astonishment as the fish, immediately on finding itself hooked, swam at top speed towards him and shot up the gravel bank to his feet. The battle was over before it had even begun and the vicar was only concerned that no one would believe his tale of this and his earlier extraordinary fish.

THE ROAD TO GODLINESS

AFRICA, 1839

The early days of the Victorian era saw a boom in the numbers of British Christians determined to become missionaries. Partly this was because Britain was still a devout country, but it also had a great deal to do with the fact that the growing British Empire brought officials increasingly into contact with people whose beliefs were seen as completely unacceptable by their new – British – rulers. In these multicultural times it is difficult to comprehend the extent to which those who built the British Empire assumed that the rest of the world had to be brought round to the British, Christian way of doing things. But as well as Christianity, we took cricket to the ends of the Earth not just because we liked playing it, but because we assumed it would have a civilising influence on the 'savages' we encountered. The record of Christianity and cricket as tools of Empire is well recognised, but in a few forgotten corners fishing, too, was seen as something that the natives of Africa, India and beyond might benefit from. Colonel Sandford Wilkes Sandford is a case in point. Having seen service in many parts of the Empire he eventually became a civilian administrator in various parts of Africa.

By the standards of the day Colonel Sandford Wilkes Sandford was not a particularly eccentric man. However, even in the most arid parts of Africa he was rarely seen without a beautifully made – but tiny – cane fly fishing rod.

It had been specially built by one of London's finest makers for brook fishing and was what we today would call a travel rod. It was made in six short sections so that it could be carried easily and for 40 years after it was made it went everywhere with the colonel. He travelled widely in Africa, sent hither and thither by the British administration. Wherever he could he tried to find out if it was possible to catch the fish in the local rivers using his six-piece travelling rod and something resembling a fly. He tied all sorts of extraordinary flies using local materials and had a notable success with a fly that was meant to resemble a dung beetle.

At some stage in his career Colonel Sandford Wilkes Sandford decided that fishing was not just something to which he should devote his own life. Instead he decided that the way to Godliness and British Christian virtues was not through cricket but through fly fishing. Cricket hadn't worked in his part of Africa and besides he didn't like it much himself anyway. Thus began his enthusiasm for the civilising influence of dry-fly fishing. He helped local tribesmen to make rudimentary fly rods from local trees, made line from woven tapered pieces of a local vine-like plant and taught the locals to make old English flies – like Greenwell's Glory and Bloody Butcher. Reels were a bit of a problem but Colonel Sandford Wilkes Sandford was a man who refused to be beaten so he spent months trying to make a fly reel from local hardwoods. He had some success and then showed the local tribesmen how to do it and although the reels were large and rather crude-looking they did work.

A more conventional missionary described what must have been Colonel Sandford Wilkes Sandford's finest hour. The Colonel was spotted down at the river with more than a hundred local tribesmen. They stood patiently in a line along the riverbank while the colonel walked up and down behind them pausing occasionally to offer a bit of advice or a helping hand to someone. When he'd walked the full length of the line the colonel returned to his original position and climbed on to a large rock, which gave him a good view of the men. Once in position he shouted 'Check flies!' in a loud voice, followed by 'Rods to two o'clock!'

Immediately the men stood to attention and held their makeshift rods pointing forward over the river and slightly raised.

Then came the colonel's voice again: 'Lift!' he shouted and more than a hundred makeshift rods were lifted smartly until they were just behind the vertical. 'And pause!' came the booming voice of the colonel. The makeshift vine-lines sailed out behind the better casters while others got themselves in a terrible tangle.

'And punch!' shouted the colonel. The rods came forward smartly and one or two men even managed to get their lines out across the water. Most of the rest were by now struggling with great loops of line festooned around their heads. Others were tangled in the bankside bushes. The colonel was delighted. He tried the experiment several more times and decided that several of the men had real potential as fly casters. The fly fishing lesson continued for an hour or more and then the men were marched off to church, and for the next year or two the same ritual was enacted every Sunday morning. There is no record of how the local tribesmen felt about all this, but the colonel was heard to say that one or two of his fly fishers would not by any means disgrace themselves if they ever happened to receive an invitation to fish the finest English chalkstream.

SWIMMING WITH THE FISH

ENGLAND, 1850

Frank Buckland, the son of the Dean of Westminster, was an obsessive collector of stuffed and live animals. When one of his live animals died – it might be a hippopotamus or a mouse – he usually ate it. He died in his early fifties, his life almost certainly shortened by his experiments in taxidermy. He developed some extremely effective ways to preserve dead animals, but he did it using highly poisonous chemicals that seriously damaged his health. When he wasn't stuffing animals Buckland spent his time fishing for trout and salmon. Fishing was a pursuit he'd started while at Winchester school. It had often got him into serious trouble because whenever he felt like it he would set off for the riverbank without telling anyone. When he returned he was invariably thrashed but it never dampened his enthusiasm. He was also often found asleep with a dead trout or a barbel lying next to him. He was interested at an early age in the process of putrefaction and kept dead fish and other animals until they rotted away.

In middle age Buckland's knowledge of fish – live and dead – had developed to such an extent that he was appointed Her Majesty's Inspector of Fisheries. On one never to be forgotten day he put up a sign by a weir that was still waiting for a salmon ladder to be built into it. The sign, designed for the benefit of any fish stuck below the weir, read: 'No road at present over the weir. Go downstream, take the first turning to the right and you will find good travelling water upstream and no jumping required.'

Buckland was a fanatical fisherman and after checking the weir and putting up his sign he set off to fish. Baffled by his lack of success, he stripped off – it was a very cold day in February – and lowered himself into the fastest part of the river to see what it felt like to be a salmon.

When he climbed out he was heard to mumble: 'Good God! How on earth do they do it?'

This dip into the freezing water combined with his reckless use of numerous noxious substances led Buckland to an early grave. He died aged just 54. On his deathbed fish were still on his mind and his last words were: 'God is so good, so very good, to the little fishes that I do not believe he would let their inspector suffer shipwreck.'

FLYING FISH

ENGLAND, 1866

The winds that sweep across East Anglia often originate in the northern wastes of Russia, high up in the Arctic Circle, which explains why easterly winds have a reputation for such intense cold. But these winds very occasionally bring something far more extraordinary than freezing weather.

For a keen angler fishing the wide, pike-filled Norfolk Broads in the mid-1860s the ice-cold easterlies that blew one winter's morning actually saved the day.

Our fisherman, who was the village barber, decided for the first time in many years to shut up shop on a Saturday. He was a religious man who did not like to fish on Sundays and he worried that his business would suffer if he took too many weekdays and Saturdays off, but this meant he had very little time to fish, and fishing – especially for pike – was his passion. At last he could stand it no longer. He let it be known around the village that he would not be open for business this coming Saturday and he carefully prepared his tackle for the big day.

Saturday dawned bright and cold but with a terrific wind. As he made his way across the field to his favourite mere, he noticed several trees had been knocked down. It was just after dawn and with the wind already howling about his ears he feared it might get worse as the day wore on. But there was nothing for it. He'd waited months for this outing and a bit of wind was not going to put him off.

By the time he reached the lake some 50 minutes later the wind had reached hurricane force and even the barber's determination began to crumble. The truth was he was afraid. He could barely stay on his feet and it was only the fact that he knew of a corner that was heavily protected by a copse of thick-grown trees that prevented him abandoning the whole trip. He reached the secluded corner of the lake where a low tree-covered mound immediately behind the water did indeed provide some protection from the gale. The wind was still deafening but it was coming from behind and the trees dissipated much of its force. The barber breathed a sigh of relief and began to set up his tackle. He knew this was usually a poor corner of the mere for fishing. It looked fishy enough, but he had never had much luck fishing it on calmer days. Perhaps the storm that had brought him to this quiet corner would also bring the fish.

The morning passed uneventfully, but his dead-fish bait, heavily weighted and lying perhaps 50 yards (45.7m) out on the bottom of the lake, never moved. The gale seemed to grow more violent by the minute, but the barber was determined to take something home for his supper and if a pike came across his bait he was sure it would take it. Two o'clock came and still nothing. The barber began to think it really was time to admit defeat and set off for home while there was still light. He decided to have a last cast and began to reel in. Just at that moment he felt the first few stings as a terrific hailstorm began. He had taken his hat off and noticed immediately that, driven hard by the wind, the hailstones hurt like mad when they hit him. He dropped his rod and trotted quickly up the mound behind him and into the trees. From this more sheltered spot he saw the hailstones churn the lake to foam. They bounced off his tackle where it lay untended at the side of the lake. The barber was astonished at the size of the hailstones – they were as big as marbles and seemed to get bigger with every passing minute.

Then an especially big marble landed just 6ft (1.8m) from him and, hardly believing his eyes, he noticed that the lump of ice wasn't round at all. It was far more oval in shape. He went closer and saw that it was in fact a small fish. As he bent to pick it up he noticed similar small fish lying here and there along the bank and then one or two more fell from the sky in front of him. In fact all across the lake small silver fish were falling out of the sky.

The barber was sure that no one would believe that he'd seen fish falling out of the sky so he collected several dozen and put them in his fishing basket. He then packed his tackle away and set off for home. He need not have worried about being believed for the story of the fish falling out of the sky reached the village before he did.

In fact, what the barber had witnessed was a rare but well-documented phenomenon. Very strong winds will occasionally lift small, whitebait-sized fish from the ocean and then deposit them on the land. The barber dined out for many years on the story and he relished the tale of how one stormy day he'd made a good bag of fish without catching a thing.

IMPOSSIBLE TROUT

SCOTLAND, 1877

For five years they had tried to catch him. For five years they had failed. Groups of men were known to sit up half the night devising plans to catch him, but however ingenious the plans they always failed. The object of all the fuss was a large brown trout that had taken up residence in an insignificant tributary of one of Scotland's best-known salmon rivers. In the land where the salmon is king such a fish, being a trout, would have not warranted much attention, but as the trout grew bigger it began to annoy the locals who said: 'Och, it's only an old trout. We should get it out and knock it on the head.' But of course that was easier said than done and no sooner had they decided to try to catch him than they themselves were hooked on what for a very long time seemed a hopeless quest.

By the time he was estimated to weigh as much as 7–8lb (3.2–3.6kg) there was hardly a moment in the week when someone or other wasn't staring over the bridge and down into his lair. He would drift in and out from under his favourite boulder looking for titbits brought down by the stream and looked like nothing so much as a miniature submarine.

The reason he was so difficult to catch was that he was in a deep part of an extremely narrow stream with sheer banks nearly 20ft (6.1m) high on either side. He'd been hooked several times and played to a standstill, but he was too heavy to be lifted from the water and no landing net could reach him. One or two anglers tried using line that would be strong enough to lift him bodily up the steep banks but line strong enough to achieve this was so thick that the trout spotted it and refused to have anything to do with the juicy bait dangling from the end of it.

Then came the day when one of the regulars at the bridge gossiping sessions decided he would catch that old trout if it was the last thing he did. The fisherman was an engineer by profession so he contacted a friend who was a metalworker and asked him to make a very long, very light landing net handle. In fact when fully extended the landing net handle measured a little over 19ft (5.8m), but even at that great length it would only just be long enough to reach the fish. With net in hand, rod at the ready and gillie by his side the fisherman set off for the stream. He had the strongest cast he dared risk if he was to have any chance of hooking the fish in the first place, but on this day luck was with him and 20 minutes after he'd started to fish he hooked the monster trout. Now, from the top of that steep bank it was very difficult to play that trout. Twice it almost reached the narrow falls a little further downstream. If it had crossed the falls down into the next pool it would have been lost, but the gut held and soon the giant trout was wallowing quietly beneath the tip of the rod. It was time to bring the great gangling landing net into play. The gillie extended the net as far as it would go and lowered it towards the fish. It reached the water and the massive trout began to slide over the rim. Just then, as often happens with big wild trout, it gave a savage lunge, twisted back out of the net and made a powerful rush for freedom. The sudden burst of activity was so unexpected that fisherman and gillie jumped with alarm, slipped into each other at the top of the bank and, losing their footing, fell headlong into the stream.

Luckily the water was deep at this particular point and both men surfaced spluttering and cursing but otherwise unharmed. There was no way the two men could climb the bank and they knew that shouting for help would be unlikely to do much good. There was only one thing for it – they had to swim down across the narrow falls into the lower pool where the banks were less steep. Here they clambered out and set off without a word back along the road to the village. Changed into dry clothes the fisherman returned to the river an hour later to find his landing net and rod. Both were broken, the landing net handle beyond repair.

That same evening the fisherman could be seen striding purposefully along the road to the high-banked stream. This time he carried just two items: a fishing rod and a shotgun. When he reached the river he tied on a very light cast and a hook with three fresh lobworms on it. He lowered the bait into the pool. Nothing happened. He waited nearly two hours and still nothing. Clearly the experience of having two fully grown men land in the pool had been too much for the trout and he was not in a feeding mood.

But every day for the next week the fisherman returned to the stream with his rod, his worms and his shotgun and every day he waited. At last the big trout took the bait. The fisherman played him carefully and when at last he wallowed quietly immediately below the rod tip the fisherman bent down carefully, picked up his shotgun – which had been loaded all the time – slipped off the safety catch and fired directly at the trout. There was a huge splash, but when the water became calm again there was not a sign of the trout and from that day on he was never seen again in the steep pool or anywhere else. He must have been killed but it was odd that his body was never found. The fisherman never quite got over his disappointment at not carrying the fish home – indeed it was said he had given up fishing and taken up golf instead.

MAD PIKE MAN
IRELAND, 1880

Angling breeds eccentrics, but few can have been more dotty and obsessed with fish than the fisherman writer John Bickerdyke met in a remote corner of Ireland in 1880.

Returning from a day's fishing to the little house at the eastern end of the glen where he'd been staying, Bickerdyke first noticed an unusual rod and reel leaning against the wall in the hall. At its point the rod was as thick as a finger and the reel, in heavy gunmetal, was at least 8in (20.3cm) in diameter. But it was the line that really caught Bickerdyke's eye: 'I have towed a canoe up the Thames with cord less thick,' he exclaimed.

Bickerdyke was about to ask the lady of the house about the tackle he had seen when the door burst open and in came a short, wiry old man with iron-grey hair and clad in a shabby suit of tweeds that might have been young half a century earlier. He carried another giant rod and reel and a huge basket.

He took no notice at all of Bickerdyke, but shouted at the woman. 'Bring me the scales. Quick!'

With trembling hands he opened the basket and tipped on to the floor the biggest pike Bickerdyke had ever seen. The lady of the house proceeded to weigh the fish and as she did this the old man hopped about in an ecstasy of excitement.

'Is it? Is it?' he asked again and again.

'No, he isn't,' came the reply. 'He's 5lb [2.3kg] short.'

With that the old man fainted.

The lady of the house said that the old man hadn't eaten for two days. As they tried to lift him he woke and gazed in anguish at the pike, which now lay discarded on the ground.

'Only 35lb [15.9kg],' he muttered. 'Only 35lb. But I will have him one day. I will have him.'

The lady of the house returned with a huge glass of a drink made from milk and brandy, which seemed to revive the old man. It was then for the first time that he noticed Bickerdyke. The lady of the house, a Mrs O'Day, made the introductions.

'This gentleman has come for the trout fishing,' she explained to the old man who continued to look suspiciously at Bickerdyke.

'You're sure he's not here for the pike,' he said.

Once he was satisfied that Bickerdyke had no interest in pike fishing the two men ate their supper together and then retired to the fireside to chat.

Bickerdyke discovered that his companion was an Englishman who had lived for almost half a century in Ireland, spending virtually every day fishing, and always for pike.

Bickerdyke asked the old man why the weighing of the pike had troubled him so much.

The old man replied: 'From my youth I was an enthusiastic fisherman – I caught gudgeon in the Thames, salmon in Norway, trout in the Test and huge grayling in the Hampshire Avon. I fished whenever and wherever I could and nothing, however large or small, came amiss to me. But one thing I had never caught – a really big pike. This nettled me because I'd read so many tales of huge – particularly Irish – pike.

'One day I read in an English paper a letter from an Irish tackle dealer asking why more English anglers didn't try their hand at Irish fishing. It was the best in Europe he said and there was so much of it. He also wrote that 35–40lb

(13.6–18.1kg) pike were common in Irish loughs. I told my friends that I would catch a 40lb pike. They laughed and said it could not be done, that no such beast existed, so I made a bet with them that I would go to Ireland and catch a fish of that weight and that I would not return until I had done so.

'Anyway, I wrote to the tackle dealer, not knowing that in the week after his letter had been published he had died. His wife replied saying she did not know exactly which loughs he had been referring to when he talked about the abundance of pike in Irish waters. Frustrated, I put a letter in the sporting newspapers asking for information and I received many replies. Some were genuine and helpful I am sure but one or two interested parties – keen pike fishermen I mean – deliberately wrote, I suspect, to set me on the wrong trail.

'I heard of a huge pike caught from Lough Derg and of others from other places here and there. I tried all the Shannon loughs and Corrib and Cullen. I caught many pike but none of 40lb, and the more difficult it seemed to become the more determined was I. And I shall succeed yet. That pike there,' and here he pointed to the huge fish still lying on the floor, 'that is the biggest I have yet caught. In fact it is the biggest I have yet seen caught anywhere by anyone.

'That fish in fact is my second disappointment. At Athlone I thought I had succeeded. I caught a huge fish and took him to the station to have him weighed. The scales dipped to 43lb (19.5kg), but a gentleman standing by began prodding the fish with his stick. He said he thought there was something odd and we should cut the fish open. We did so and found a mass of lead shot which my scoundrel of a boatman had evidently poured down his throat in order to earn the reward I had promised him if we caught a heavy fish.

'But at last I have found a truly monstrous pike – the catching of him is only a matter of time. Not a quarter of a mile (400m) from this house,' here he lowered his voice to a whisper, 'is a deep reedy lake. The priest has a boat on it that he frequently lends me. The other evening I was rowing across the lake when something struck the boat with such force that I was thrown from the seat and nearly capsized. It was in deep water and there are no rocks in that lake. I believe I had rowed on to a pike as big as a calf.'

On hearing this, Bickerdyke suggested that they try the lake together the very next day.

'But then you might catch him and not I,' came the reply. With that the old man began to look at Bickerdyke with a distinctly malevolent eye. A long silence ensued and then the old man asked if Bickerdyke was aware that he had been talking to the Emperor of Germany. Bickerdyke said he had not realised. More silence and then the two men settled down to sleep, one on either side of the fire.

As Bickerdyke began to doze off he heard movements and then a voice close to his ear.

'Hang me if I don't believe you are a pike. I'll have a hook into you tomorrow morning. Goodnight.'

Bickerdyke concluded that his companion had been driven mad by his long search for a giant pike.

Too afraid to sleep Bickerdyke waited until first light, left the money he owed his landlady on a table and then sped away off over the moor. He did not return.

SEEING EYE TO EYE

ENGLAND, 1880

Perch are famously voracious fish. Throw even the soil in which worms have been kept into the water and shoals of little perch will congregate and you will catch one every cast. Bigger perch are far more wary, however, but they will attack almost anything – even fish much bigger than themselves.

The splendidly named Victorian naturalist H. Cholmondeley Pennell was an ardent fan of the perch and he travelled widely in pursuit of really big specimens. On a trip to the Lake District where he fished long and hard, day and night, in pursuit of a record-breaking fish, he encountered a most remarkable example of the perch's outlandish appetite.

He'd just landed a very reasonable perch. It was a good fish, but nowhere near the monster on which he'd set his heart. He gently unhooked the fish, but the angle at which the hook had penetrated the side of the fish's mouth meant that, in removing the hook he accidentally also removed the poor creature's eye.

Horrified, Cholmondeley Pennell thought it would be best to knock the fish on the head, but he was a skilled naturalist and knew from experience that fish are endowed with remarkable powers of recovery. He gave the fish the benefit of the doubt and gently released it into the lake. It swam off apparently quite unperturbed by the loss of one eye.

Cholmondeley Pennell then discovered that he had run out of worms, but it was evening and time to pack up anyway. It was then that he noticed the perch eye still stuck on his hook. He decided to take his rod down after packing away his tackle bag and other bits and pieces. He swung his float tackle – with the eye still attached to his hook – out into the lake and then set about packing his bag. A few moments later he looked up and noticed that his float had disappeared. Thinking it must have drifted into a reed bed he lifted his rod only to find that he had hooked a fish. It was another perch and about the size of the last.

Cholmondeley Pennell was delighted and amazed because the only bait on the hook was the previous perch's eye, but amazement turned to wonder when he discovered that this perch now flapping angrily in his net had only one eye! Not only was it a cannibal, but it was prepared, not ten minutes after being caught the first time, to eat its own eye!

DIFFICULT TO STOMACH
CEYLON, 1882

Major F. Powell Hopkins wrote a wonderful, but now forgotten book about his adventures in modern-day Sri Lanka at the end of the nineteenth century. With his pith helmet and enormous jodhpurs he seems to have cut a striking figure. But when he went fishing he caused an even greater stir because he insisted on wearing the tweeds he wore when fishing in Scotland.

Such was his enthusiasm for angling that when he caught a fish he insisted that his fellow officers should eat it. As the months went by the number of fish he caught and brought to the mess increased and the groans of his fellow officers increased, but no one could quite pluck up the courage to say something to him. The days wore on, the number of trout grew ever greater and the officers grew ever more weary of this endless diet of fish. They gorged on trout and other local species until the day came when there was a serious risk of mutiny.

But it was the major himself who saved the day by catching a few more fish than was absolutely necessary. He'd gone out to his favourite trout fishing pool on the local river specifically to catch fish for his officers. Stocks were getting low and he was convinced his men would be upset if he did not continue to keep them well supplied. After little more than an hour he realised that the trout were simply not interested. But what was this? Some other species – silvery and highly acrobatic – had taken up residence in the pool. For a while the major just watched as, under the far bank, these elegant-looking fish rose to take an occasional berry as it fell from an overhanging bush.

These were feeding fish and the major was determined to take a few back to camp. He made his way along the river until he found a similar bush to the one he'd seen on the far bank. He collected a pocketful of berries and returned to his favourite pool. Over the next two hours he simply couldn't put a foot wrong. Every cast produced a superb, hard-fighting barbel-like fish. He hadn't a clue what these fish were but they rose eagerly to his bait and he caught dozens. The men would be delighted. That evening he struggled back to camp with a huge basket of these unidentified fish. The officers praised his skill, but suggested – with enormous generosity, thought the major – that it was time the other ranks enjoyed the benefits of the major's skill with rod and line.

Thus it was that the major's company dined that evening on a new kind of fish stew. The major, still in his huge shorts and pith helmet, watched with satisfaction as the men helped themselves. In the morning he was not quite so happy. Every single man in the company had gone down with dysentery. They had to be taken to hospital and were out of action for nearly two months. Two men were so badly affected that they were shipped home to England. The major, to the delight of the officers, was forbidden ever to bring fish back to the camp again.

BEST OF FRIENDS
SCOTLAND, 1885

An angler on a stretch of water was fishing quite happily when a giant of a man approached him along the bank in full Highland dress shouting and angrily brandishing a large wooden club. The Highland chieftain – which is what he looked like – was furious. So much so in fact that what he was saying was almost incomprehensible.

Before the by now terrified angler lay the water, too deep to wade; behind him approached the ferocious foe. The fisherman expected at any moment to be hurled into the water by his fierce assailant, whose anger knew no bounds when he was informed by the fisherman that he, the fisherman, understood the visitor at the Dunalastair Hotel had the right of fishing in the river.

It would have been worth a small fortune to have witnessed that interview. The poor fisherman hadn't a clue what to say beyond offering the ordinary apologies. But he took the wisest course when he produced a well-filled flask, and proceeded to lubricate his apologies with neat whisky; until so effectual did the method prove that the enemy's wrath was entirely mollified.

Within half an hour, such is the power of the single malt, the two men had become the greatest of friends. And then it was that the Highlander, upon learning the name of his unconscious offender, granted to him and his progeny until the third or fourth generation the right of fishing the water whenever and wherever they chose.

COACHING THE POACHER

SCOTLAND, 1888

Salmon poaching on a small scale was once an accepted fact of Scottish life. But in the days when a man might regularly spear a couple of fish from the shallows to feed his hungry family, salmon stocks were high and the effects of poaching were negligible. But that said, poaching was a serious offence in law and it could lead not just to a court appearance but to the loss of one's job and even one's home. In remoter areas the fear of being caught would have been slight since there really was very little chance of bumping into a riverkeeper or gillie, but it did happen. On at least one occasion a poacher was caught by a gillie and refused to run away. Perhaps the most exceptional example of this happened one afternoon on the River Awe.

The local gillie had taken two fisherman out that morning but they had grown tired and returned to their hotel at lunchtime. The gillie went back to the river to enjoy a few hours' undisturbed fishing on his own account. Meanwhile a poor crofter who lived a few miles from the river decided that he would go down and help himself to a salmon if the coast was clear. The poacher reached the river before the gillie. He was not the worst sort of poacher for he enjoyed the process of catching his salmon and refused ever to indulge in anything as unsporting as a spear. No, when he went fishing for salmon he used a rod and line just like the grandest English aristocrat. The difference was that instead of a fly he used a worm. He reached a pool in which he'd seen a number of salmon the previous evening. First cast he hooked a giant of a fish and he was experienced enough to know that it would not be beaten in less than an hour. He looked about and could see no one. He played the fish as hard as he dared. Ten minutes passed, twenty. Still the salmon charged up and down the pool as if this tugging at its jaw was no more than a minor irritation.

After an hour the crofter glanced up and saw sitting on a rock on the opposite bank and smoking his pipe – the gillie. The two men knew each other so there was no point in making a run for it. And besides, the crofter knew he could not bear to lose this fish. The gillie stared hard at the crofter but never said a word. The crofter, pale as a sheet, continued to play his fish. As the battle continued, the crofter became aware of a strange grumbling sound that seemed to be coming from the gillie over the water. All he could make out in the gillie's ramblings were odd curses and his own name. The crofter knew that the gillie would very likely evict him for this, but he said nothing. What could he say? He continued to play his salmon and all the while he could hear the gillie's curses. Then the fish made a sudden lunge for a huge rock that stuck up halfway across the stream. 'Mind yon rock!' shouted the gillie. 'D'ye no ken the risk? Lift up your rod man!'

The astonished crofter obeyed and the line just cleared the obstruction. The gillie had saved the day for a man who was poaching his river. The crofter tried to start up an apologetic-sounding conversation. He shouted across that he'd only been after something for his supper but that when he'd hooked the big fish he couldn't bear to break his line. He shouted across that all men were brothers in sport.

But none of it made any difference. The gillie had returned to his mumbling and cursing, and now the crofter noticed that the gillie was cursing himself for helping the crofter. And that is how it continued for the next two hours. Each time the crofter looked as if he might lose his fish, the gillie stopped grumbling and cursing and shouted across words of advice. When the crisis was over he returned to his grumbling and his malevolent staring. At last the crofter slid his net under a salmon that weighed at least 30lb (13.6kg). He was elated but how could he enjoy his victory when he knew that he would lose his job and his home? He decided there was simply no point attempting an escape and with the fish in his net he walked the three-quarters of a mile (1.2km) to the nearest bridge, crossed over and then walked dejectedly back along the opposite bank to the rock where the gillie was still sitting. As he came into view he heard the gillie's voice.

'You'd never have landed him without my help, would ye?'

The crofter agreed that the gillie's help had indeed been invaluable.

'It was my knowledge of the stones that saved ye. My knowledge of the river.'

'It was indeed,' replied the crofter in as humble a voice as he could manage.

'I believe it was my knowledge of the pool that got him out safe. My knowledge of your tackle... my advice... my skill...'

What on earth was he getting at, wondered the crofter?

'In fact I believe it is my fish,' said the gillie finally.

The crofter suddenly realised what was being proposed. If he agreed that the gillie had caught this fish, he would be let off the crime of having poached the river. This was a terrible dilemma. The crofter knew he had to choose between giving up the biggest fish of his life – and one of the best from the river – and losing his home. With a sinking heart he recognised it was no choice at all. He had to give up the fish and so he agreed that he had indeed only helped land the gillie's fish. The gillie took possession of the salmon and the crofter set off for home. For weeks afterwards he had to bite his tongue as tales of the gillie's huge fish spread up and down the river and on more than one occasion the crofter wished he'd taken his fish and given up his home.

WISE OLD TROUT
ENGLAND, 1890

He was an old, wise and very big trout, and had his headquarters opposite a clubhouse on a certain famous stream. Many a fly had passed over his venerable head. Long-standing club members remembered when, years before, he had been hooked on a piece of bread, but he quickly wound the line round a stump, extracted the hook and was rising to some natural flies half an hour later.

New members used to bet that they would catch him. The old members took their bets and then took their money.

It was an aggravating feature in the clubhouse trout's behaviour that nothing would frighten him. A badly presented fly or line falling in a great heap close by him had no effect at all. He took absolutely no notice, but with this lack of fear came the cunning of a hawk.

One day a man with little experience of trout fishing joined the club. He had spent his fishing life to date in pursuit of chub, carp and barbel and was an expert at catching fish that took bait. He, like the rest, said he thought he could catch the trout – and he was convinced he could do it using an artificial fly. The old members laughed and took his bets, as was their custom with newcomers.

It was August. One sultry evening the new member came to the club armed with a pea-shooter and a tin filled with bluebottles. Was he going to catch the trout with a pea-shooter? No, he was only going to begin to catch him –

the operation might take some time, he explained. He went down to the river and stood on the bank opposite the clubhouse. He put the pea-shooter to his lips, selected a fat, juicy dead bluebottle and puffed it out of the tube. The bluebottle was big enough and heavy enough to shoot out across the river and land in front of the fish. It was taken, of course, as everything eatable from a trout's point of view was taken. The fish had a rare supper that evening. Bluebottle after bluebottle shot out over his head and he sipped them down.

The following day the new member repeated the operation. He fed the fish in this manner for more than a week; the others smiled and looked on.

'I will catch him soon,' said the new member. 'I am waiting only for wind.'

At the end of three weeks there came a day when a stiff breeze was blowing upstream. The new member appeared at the clubhouse with a long slender rod, on which was arranged a fly reel, a length of light silk line and a cast of strong gut.

The fisherman took his stand some distance below the fish, and began feeding him bluebottles as usual. Then he put a bluebottle on his hook and with considerable skill he pulled plenty of line from his reel and allowed line and fly to be lifted and blown across the river. Good luck helped the fisherman and his hooked fly landed just a yard (91.4cm) above the wily trout. As the hooked bluebottle fell on to the water the fisherman puffed out one last loose bluebottle. The loose bluebottle landed close to the hooked insect and the two drifted down towards the waiting trout.

Which would the trout take? It was an anxious moment. Had the rod been in front instead of behind him, he would have taken neither. But he did not see the rod, having no eyes in his tail.

The loose fly was sucked in and after an awful pause that seemed to last for ever, up came the big old trout again and the fly with the hook in it vanished. A second later the big trout was thrashing and leaping across the top of the water as he fought for his freedom.

He tried all his old tricks, but the big stump he'd used to escape the bread fisher had long gone. Likewise the weed, which had recently been cut back. He bored deep, he made long heart-stopping runs, but all to no avail. After ten minutes the clubhouse trout was safe in the net. The fisherman collected his winnings from the astonished members and the biggest and oldest trout ever caught from the stream found its way into a splendid glass case where it remains to this day.

THE BITER BIT

LONDON, 1890

It is rare, but not unheard of, for a fisherman to hook a fish and then, while playing it, to see it swallowed by a bigger fish, usually, in freshwater fishing, a pike. The result inevitably is that the fisherman loses everything – the original fish, the pike and of course his hook.

A letter to *The Spectator* reveals a far rarer occurrence. A man fishing the lake in Battersea Park hooked a small roach. As he reeled it in, a big perch slashed at the roach and found that it too had become attached to the angler's hook.

The perch almost certainly weighed well over 2lb (0.9kg) – very big indeed for the Battersea Lake – and the fisherman was terrified he might lose it so he played it with all the skill he could muster. But that perch was both big and very lively. It plunged repeatedly, taking line and convincing the fisherman that it would inevitably slip the hook and escape.

But no. It began to tire and a grateful fishermen thought he might at last land this remarkable specimen. The perch was perhaps 15ft (4.6m) from the net when a long, green shadow appeared as if from nowhere. Moving very quickly it seized the perch and moved like an arrow out towards the middle of the lake. The fisherman could not believe what had happened. But even more remarkable than hooking a roach, a perch and a pike all on the same tackle, was that 20 minutes later the fisherman managed to land the pike with the remains of both the perch and the roach still in its mouth.

NUTTY PROFESSOR

SCOTLAND, 1892

An eminent professor from an ancient Oxford college was on holiday in Scotland towards the end of the nineteenth century. He'd left his hotel early on this particular morning because the night before he' d heard talk in the hotel bar of the great numbers of salmon spawning in the river nearby and was determined to see them.

By nine o'clock he was standing on the edge of a likely looking pool but had not yet seen a thing. A wind got up and the professor – too set in his ways to dress for the occasion and still wearing his city suit – suddenly found his black hat whirled from his head and out into the middle of the river. Nothing daunted he pulled out a large red handkerchief, knotted it at the corners and pulled it down on his head.

After watching the pool intently for a further ten minutes without sight of a fish, he decided to try a little further downstream.

He rounded the next bend in the river and spotted a tall, well-built, but rather rough-looking man standing on a rock in the middle of the stream and apparently attempting to hit something in the water with a long stick.

'Ah,' thought the professor, 'this must be a local chap fishing for salmon.'

The man in the river – a notorious poacher – had spotted the well-dressed gentleman with the extraordinary headgear and would have given anything to be able to run away, but between him and liberty in the form of the opposite bank lay some deep and very fast-flowing water. He had no choice other than to return to the bank where stood the professor. It was either that or drown. So he hopped across the rocks and landed right at the professor's feet.

'Have you caught any salmon?' asked the professor.

The man had been all ready to make a dash for it, but judging by the old man's friendly tone and curious dress – the professor still wore his red handkerchief as a hat – he thought he must be one of those rare gentlemen who took a generous view of the poacher's art. 'I haven't even seen a fish,' he replied, 'but I think there would be a good chance of a big fish a little further upstream.'

The professor was delighted and immediately offered the man ten shillings if he would help him catch a salmon.

The poacher was astonished. Here was an apparently respectable old man – respectable apart from the strange hat – offering him a generous reward for breaking the law.

He led the professor up the river to a broad, shallow glide where two heavy fish had taken up station at the edge of the water. He showed the professor how to use his long cleek – a gaff-like instrument. Within minutes the internationally known professor of anatomy was dragging a 20lb (9.1kg) salmon up the shingle.

The professor was delighted and completely unaware that he had just committed a serious offence punishable by a prison sentence.

He was none the wiser even as eggs spilled out of the salmon. These he picked up, and examined using a pocket microscope that he dug out of a special pocket in his long coat.

Suddenly his companion grabbed the professor's arm and pulled him behind a rock.

'They're after us!' he hissed.

'Who?' asked the bewildered academic.

'Why, the police of course,' came the reply.

'But why?'

It was then that the poacher decided to explain to the professor exactly what it was they'd just done.

The professor put his head in his hands and slumped down on to a rock. But the poacher pulled him to his feet and told him that they would be caught within minutes if they stayed behind the rock. He suggested that they make their way separately across the moor. That would give them both a better chance of escape than if they stayed together.

The professor, terrified at the prospect of an appearance in the local magistrates' court, a spell in prison and the reaction of his university colleagues, ran faster than he had ever run in his life. He threw off his temporary headgear as well as his coat, but within minutes of bolting he'd been spotted by the police, who immediately gave chase.

If the professor had been a better runner he would certainly have been caught, but he quickly tired and began to stumble. Then as he came down a slight incline, which meant he was temporarily out of sight of the pursuing police, he fell down through soft heather into a deep hole between rocks. No sooner had he slipped into the hole than the heather closed over his head and when the police reached the place all they could do was stand and scratch their heads. Their quarry had been just 100 yards (91.4m) ahead of them and now he was gone.

The professor meanwhile lay there defeated and sure he was about to be taken. If he had not been so exhausted he would have attempted to climb out of his little hole and run on – and he would have been caught. But he stayed where he was and escaped retribution just in the moment when he was most likely to suffer it. The police were soon 1 mile (1.6km) away. The old man stayed put until night fell and still he did not move. Eventually in the darkness he groped his way back to the lodge where he'd been staying. He was tired, scratched and torn; he'd lost his coat, his hat, his handkerchief; his glasses were broken, his shoes were gone. He was unrecognisable as the man who'd set off for the river that morning.

He hid in his rooms for days and then went straight to the station where he caught the fast train to London. A few weeks later he was offered the job of fishery adviser to the fishery board. He declined and for the rest of his life he made a point of crossing the road every time he thought there was a chance he might be about to pass a fishmongers.

NEVER ON A SUNDAY

SCOTLAND, 1892

Two anglers – both Sassenachs – had waited at Loch Awe for a breeze for a whole week and waited in vain. On the sabbath morn there was a glorious ripple; the kind of ripple in which a trout rushes madly at the angler's fly. Fish these anglers must. But the gillie was an elder of the kirk and he turned up the whites of his eyes when they suggested he should just let them have the boat for an hour or two.

'I could nae do it, such a thing has no been done on the loch within the memory o' man.'

They offered untold bribes of silver and gold, but the gillie was obdurate, until his eyes rested on the gold sovereign held out to him. 'Nae, nae,' he said. 'I'll nae let the boat. I'm an elder of the kirk, ye ken, and a God-fearing man and it's no reasonable to expect me to consent to such a wicked proceeding, but the boat lies there in the rushes and the oars are in her. Just ye gang away doon and get in her and row awa oot the lake and I'll come doon and swear at ye, but ye must take no notice of what I say. Just row away and I'll call for the money the morn.'

ROACH ATTACK

ENGLAND, 1893

It's quite common in London to see geese flying overhead or swans. Along the Thames right into the heart of the City herons now stalk the shallows and various wildlife bodies tell us that owls roost in Parliament Square while kestrels hover above the Commercial Road.

Anywhere in the vicinity of London's bigger parks can be relied on to produce a bit of overspill wildlife and reports of ducks wandering across Kensington High Street with their ducklings coming along behind them are not unusual.

However, a local newspaper once carried a report of a far more surprising wildlife encounter in Kensington.

A gentleman was walking home from work one autumn evening. He'd got as far as halfway up Kensington Church Street when he was struck by what he described to the newspaper reporter as 'a terrific blow to the side of the head'. In fact the bump was so hard that it knocked the man out and he had to be taken to hospital.

One of the witnesses who'd helped the injured man into a local house where brandy was administered described a circumstance that almost certainly accounted for the knock-out blow. When the witness had run up to the man who'd been knocked out he spotted a large fish lying on the pavement nearby. Being a fisherman he knew that this was not the sort of fish one buys at a fishmonger's. It was in fact a roach, a common British freshwater fish, but completely inedible. The witness told the newspaper that at first he could not understand how the fish came to be lying in the street, but in helping the injured man to his feet he did not immediately have much time to think about it. But as he assisted the man in removing his coat he noticed something very odd indeed. The injured man's head and the shoulder of his coat were dusted here and there with fish scales. The scales were without question from the dead roach that had been found at the scene.

When the newspaper compiled its report on the incident they quoted a professor of zoology as saying that the man was almost certainly felled by a roach dropped by a passing bird, possibly a heron or cormorant.

Curiously, the paper noted with glee, the injured man – who made a full recovery – was called Mr Chub.

SUICIDAL SALMON

SCOTLAND, 1894

Fishing a spate river in Argyleshire at the end of one of the driest seasons in living memory, A.E. Gathorne Hardy decided to give it one last try. Hardly a fish had been caught in weeks, but on the morning in question Gathorne Hardy could hardly put a foot wrong. With his first cast into a pool that was no more than 50 yards (45.7m) long and 35 yards (32m) wide he hooked a 6lb (2.7kg) salmon. From 10.30a.m. until 5p.m. he never moved from that same pool, but in that time he hooked and landed 12 salmon. To hook 12 salmon in a succession of pools on one day would be remarkable, but to hook 12 in one pool in one day – and a relatively small pool at that – is a once in a lifetime experience.

Nothing seemed to frighten the fish; not a badly presented fly nor the thrashing of their hooked companions. One or two spots in the pool – by a rock, along a particular glide – produced a rise to the fly every cast. In fact Gathorne Hardy later said that every single cast that day produced some kind of a reaction from the fish. He was broken several times, a number of fish slipped the hook, dozens followed the fly.

Perhaps the most extraordinary thing of all was that on several occasions two salmon were being played at the same time, for Gathorne Hardy was using a light rod and two flies on his cast. He never managed to land two at the same time, but very few anglers can boast that they have ever had two salmon on the same cast, let alone do it twice in the same day.

FROG FISHING
ENGLAND, 1894

George Selwyn Marryat was a great friend of F.M. Halford, the man generally acknowledged as the inventor of dry-fly chalkstream fishing as we know it today. The Halford revolution began in the later part of the nineteenth century and was largely complete by 1900. It meant that South Country rivers like the Test, Kennet, Avon and Wylye were turned from mixed fisheries into places where every effort was made to eliminate all species bar the brown trout and, where it still existed, the salmon. Instead of fishing with wet fly one day, bait the next and dry fly the day after, all methods other than dry fly began to be considered not just unsporting but – in that uniquely Victorian way – ungentlemanly.

The new whipping rods that allowed the fisherman to false cast a heavy silk line before allowing a tiny artificial fly to land delicately on the water replaced much longer rods that had allowed the use of live insects. Coarse fish of all species went in one generation from being worthy of pursuit to being beyond the pale. But the turning of chalkstream fly fishing into something with strict, almost religiously obeyed, rules did not remove the element of fun. Halford himself was a dry, rather serious man, but Marryat liked to amuse. He was also a bit of an eccentric.

To entertain a friend's young daughter, named Daisy, he once went down to the River Kennet and told her he would hook and land a frog on a Mayfly. She of course told him this was quite impossible, but she had not reckoned with the accurate casting skills of her adult companion.

Our Victorian ancestors were very accomplished in the art of casting. Even with their relatively heavy rods and silk lines that had to be re-greased regularly they were astonishingly accurate casters. Dry-fly fishing today, with light, super-efficient equipment, is still an exceptionally difficult sport to master; for our angling ancestors it must have been nigh on impossible to become truly proficient.

But Marryat was one of the best casters of his day and when he said he would hook a frog he meant it. He tied on a Mayfly and wandered along the riverbank staring intently out over the water just as he would have done if he'd been after a trout. Daisy followed close behind.

Moments later a V-shape darted out from the reeds at the water's edge. It was a frog, swimming vigorously. The frog's progress towards the far bank began as a straight line but the current quickly turned a straight line into a difficult, constantly changing angle.

Marryat began to false cast. Back and forth went his line and with each cast he released a little more line from his reel. Then, just as the frog looked as if it had won the day, Marryat made his final forward throw and, light as thistledown, the Mayfly landed on the still swimming frog's back. The tiny hook just nicked the skin and soon the frog was being bounced unceremoniously towards Marryat.

The great event was recorded in a specially written letter, which still exists.

It said: 'Know all men by these presents that I, G.S. Marryat of The Close, Salisbury, did lawfully take and catch with the Fly known as the Mayfly in the water known as The Moon's Mill Pound in the River Kennet in the parish of Ramsbury one reptile, to wit a frog, in the presence of the undersigned this 20th day of August 1894.'

Marryat then signed the document and Daisy signed to witness the deed. The frog, much to Daisy's delight, was released unharmed.

PIG'S BLADDER

ENGLAND, 1895

An elderly academic anthropologist who had studied the peoples of the desert and of the Arctic was also a keen salmon fisherman. On one field trip to Greenland he noticed with interest the indigenous people's technique for catching seals. Having waited for hours for a seal to show itself they hurled a harpoon at the creature with a length of rope and a float attached to it. If the harpoon hit the seal it would immediately dive, but the float on the end of the line meant the hunters could follow the seal in their boat until it tired. They would then row over to the float and pull in the line with the seal on the other end of it. When the anthropologist talked to his interpreter he discovered that before the float idea occurred to them the Eskimos' ancestors had harpooned their seals and then struggled to hold on to the line while the seal made terrific runs for as much as half an hour. It took that long for the harpoon to subdue the animal. When the float idea occurred to them it made hunting a lot easier because the seal simply fought the buoyancy of the float, which was made from an inflated bladder.

The anthropologist returned to England and two weeks later set off for his annual fishing trip to the Wye. On his first day he hooked a salmon and his riverkeeper was astonished to see that no sooner had he hooked the fish than he threw his rod into the water. On the butt end of the rod was a curious-looking ball – it was, in fact, an inflated pig bladder. The anthropologist – much to the disgust of the riverkeeper – was conducting his own little fishing experiment. What he hadn't accounted for was the salmon's desire, once it was hooked, to head back towards the sea. The fisherman ran along the bank as fast as he was able but at 75 he was unfitted to the task. The float disappeared into the distance; the elderly anthropologist tripped over a rock and fell into the river. By the time he'd picked himself up again his rod, with its attached float, was nowhere to be seen. In fact despite hours of searching the rod was never found.

When he hooked his next fish around lunchtime the following day the elderly anthropologist hung on to it with a vengeance and the riverkeeper was secretly delighted at the slightly sheepish look on his face. The salmon was duly landed and the Eskimo experiment was over.

A SENSITIVE ISSUE

IRELAND, 1895

Given the amount of casting the average angler gets through in a day it is astonishing that our hospital casualty departments are not permanently full of fishermen and fisherwomen asking to have hooks removed from various parts of their anatomy. For the fact is that a fish hook is a nasty piece of equipment if it manages to snare the fisher rather than the fish.

One man who suffered badly from misplaced hooks was Major F. Powell Hopkins. He was a skilful and enthusiastic fisherman who caught dozens of different species during a long Army career that took him all over the world. In retirement he spent a great deal of time in Ireland fishing every day for months on end for salmon, trout and sea trout. Despite the fact that he was enormously experienced he was also rather clumsy, but being convinced that a British officer – even a retired British officer – was always right he tended to blame his long-suffering gillie for any mistakes. The gillie got his revenge on one unforgettable day, however.

The two men were out fishing on a lough in the West of Ireland when the major hooked a large salmon. He played the fish for 20 minutes and then drew it towards the gillie's net. It had all seemed so easy up until this point. The salmon had fought hard and there had been exciting moments when it might have got off, but it was a relief now to bring it to the net as they were unlikely to get another fish that day.

Perhaps it was this knowledge that made the major a little more complacent that he would normally have been. But whatever the reason, he discovered, while the salmon still had several feet to go to reach the net, that he had tied on a very long cast and that the last part of the cast could not be reeled in because the fly on the top dropper had jammed in the top ring of the rod.

The major couldn't walk backwards – which is what he would have done if he'd been fishing from the bank – and he had no other options. He held his rod as high as he could to keep a tight line with the salmon, but he was in a jam and he knew it. Quick as a flash he decided there was only one solution. He handed the rod to his gillie and then reached up to grab the cast near the top of the rod. The salmon was tired, which was reassuring, but the major noticed that his hook had only a very light hold on the fish's jaw. He began to pull the fish towards him, hand over hand along the gut cast. With just 3ft (0.9m) of line to go before he could get his fingers in the salmon's gills and whip it out, disaster struck. The salmon had clearly had time to recover a little and seeing the major bending so close it decided to make one last bid for freedom. With a flick of its powerful tail – the fish must have weighed nearly 20lb (9.1kg) – it plunged deep beneath the boat pulling the cast through the major's hands. It was at this moment that the gillie heard a piercing scream and on looking across he saw the major hopping about in the end of the boat like a demented thing. The major was also shouting and cursing. He was clearly in great pain, but the gillie was baffled and could see no reason for the fuss. But then he realised what had happened.

As the gut had been yanked out of the major's hands the top fly – the one that had jammed in the rod rings and started all the trouble in the first place – had caught the major in the front of his trousers. From listening to the major's cries the gillie quickly surmised that the hook had not just penetrated the major's trousers in the region of his buttons. Worse – much worse – the hook had quite clearly hooked something highly sensitive inside the major's trousers. By this time the major was howling in pain and dancing a curious jig. He'd managed to catch hold of the cast again to stop the tugs of the salmon inflicting even more pain and injury on him, but the gut was cutting the major's hands. It was the only time in his life that the major had wished desperately to lose a fish, but despite everything the gut held and the salmon continued to thrash on the end of the line.

In the instant the gillie understood what had taken place he involuntarily laughed. Incensed, the major took a swing and boxed the gillie with his free hand. The punch winded the gillie who fell awkwardly into the back of the boat. The violent rocking caused by the fall made the salmon panic and the major's hands and groin began to suffer again.

It took five minutes for the gillie to get back on his feet and cut the line. The major sat silent and scowling as the gillie rowed them back to the bank. He was furious with the gillie, but knew that the story would be all over the village if he did not apologise for his behaviour. At last the solution came to him. He offered the gillie a full bottle of whisky on condition that not a word of the day's affair was breathed to anyone. The gillie shook on it and the two men agreed to meet again in the morning for another day on the lough.

THE VICAR'S RECORD-BREAKER

SCOTLAND, 1898

It was on Loch Awe, just opposite the big hotel, that Mr Marjoribanks, a church minister, had his memorable battle with a salmon.

The weather had been dry that year for weeks. The head of the loch was full of salmon waiting for a spate to allow them to pass up the Orchy and as a result a good many boats were out daily, trolling backwards and forwards, for the chance of a fish. This, of course, necessitated the gillie (who was also the best head-waiter in Scotland) keeping a sharp look-out from the terrace, in order to apprise the visitors at the earliest moment, should such an exciting event occur as the landing of a salmon.

It therefore goes without saying that, when the hotel was informed by the keen-eyed gillie that the worthy minister was actually playing a heavy fish within sight of the windows, a large crowd gathered as if by magic upon the terrace. Every point of vantage was quickly secured – many of the spectators being armed with opera-glasses, or other instruments for assisting the ordinary vision. The minister was in charge of the local Wee Frees, that strict Presbyterian sect, and he was not popular with everyone. That said, few in the crowd wished him anything but success with what was clearly a fine salmon, for the minister had not recently had much luck on the river.

It was soon recognised that the fish was an exceptionally heavy one, for it continued to maintain its position deep down in the water. Indeed, the fish showed little signs of making any decided movement beyond a constant revolution in a small circle, accompanied by a perpetual tugging of the line.

As the minutes slowly passed, the anticipation of the onlookers became intense. The enforced inactivity began to tell palpably on their nerves, so that, when a suggestion was made that possibly the minister had no gaff in the boat, the idea was accepted with the greatest avidity. Many eager hands rushed off to secure an implement with which to land the monster – anything to allay the numbing sense of inaction that had well-nigh overmastered the crowd.

In a very few minutes a gaff was forthcoming, and a gillie despatched to the assistance of the hero of the hour, who, with grim and set face, still held on to the giant fish.

Presently, amid breathless excitement among the spectators on the terrace above, the minister exerted all his power, and gradually wound up the unseen leviathan to the surface of the water. As more pressure was brought to bear upon the fish, the line appeared to gyrate ever more rapidly. At last the top of the trace became visible, and a shout of dismay burst from the agonised audience, as with a mighty CLOOP a big black bottle bounded out of the water, attached to the now unhappy minister's phantom minnow.

It was an abominable piece of bad luck. There was a small hole near the bottom of the neck of the bottle, in which one of the treble hooks had caught, thus causing the bottle to tug and gyrate in the water, for all the world like a heavy and sulky fish.

It was adding insult to injury when some wag noised it abroad that the minister had 'taken to the bottle'.

AN EXHIBITION OF MONSTERS

IRELAND, 1898

John Bickerdyke, a well-known Victorian fisherman, was staying in a remote Irish hotel towards the end of the nineteenth century. One evening he heard his landlord tell his wife that he needed to go out on the lough to catch fish for their guests' supper. Being usually glad of an excuse to go fishing, Bickerdyke begged to join in the search after trout and the landlord lent him one of his boats. Leaving the landlord to fish round a little bay, Bickerdyke set off to a distant corner of the lough, where he had often seen large trout rising.

It took some 20 minutes to reach the chosen spot, and by that time a slight favouring ripple, which might have helped Bickerdyke to a fish, had died away. Dark clouds were gathering and just as he reached his fishing ground he heard distant thunder rumbling along the mountains. Then happened one of the strangest things he had ever seen in his life.

A few fine spots of rain began to fall and with them came vast swarms of small black flies. Hardly had these touched the water than, all around, enormous trout began to show themselves and swim about with their back fins out of the water. The water was quite literally boiling with wild brown trout, the smallest of which Bickerdyke estimated at 6lb (2.7kg). The biggest were all well over 10lb (4.5kg). Their writhing antics seemed to cover every inch of the water for hundreds of yards in every direction.

Bickerdyke, shaking with excitement, was convinced he would land a basketful, but despite all his efforts not one fish would look at his flies. He began to realise that he was doomed to failure, but then, when he had absolutely given up all hope, a massive fish rose, took his fly and then lunged for the bottom of the lake.

Bickerdyke said later that he had never fought such a battle in his life before and never had he been so terrified of losing a fish. But luck was with him and soon the giant fish, which weighed a little over 10lb (4.5kg), was in the net. In that instant, as if on some invisible signal, the lough surface died to quiet and the exceptional rise was over.

FEARLESS FOE?

ENGLAND, 1900

J.W. Martin, known as the Trent Otter, was an enormously entertaining angling writer. Very popular in his day, he is now pretty much forgotten by all but a few enthusiasts. His accounts of fishing days are especially entertaining because he avoids the common trap of simply telling you how to do it. His books are filled with anecdote and incident and he made great efforts to record the bizarre and unusual.

Among many strange experiences he recalls the day he set off to fish for pike on a remote river in the West Country. Now Martin was an experienced pike fisherman who had caught thousands of pike in a career lasting more than 50 years. He had seen pike virtually commit suicide in the rush to engulf a well-presented deadbait. On other occasions he noted pike that almost chased a lure into the boat. And though there were days when nothing would tempt even the smallest pike, the general rule was and is that pike are fearless and will attack anything that comes close to them – including other pike much bigger than themselves. This accounts for the occasional discovery of pike dead with other pike wedged in their mouths. What happens is that, say, a 10lb (4.5kg) pike attacks another 10lb pike. The attacking fish finds he can't swallow the pike in his mouth but neither can he spit it out. He then dies and so, of course, does the pike wedged halfway down his throat.

All of this was well known to Martin when he fished that

forgotten West Country water, and as his boat rode out across the placid, early morning river he had high expectations of a good day's fishing. Numerous pike had been spotted by a friend of Martin's in the days leading up to the great man's visit. The pike – one or two were estimated at well over 25lb (11.3kg) – had taken up residence in a shallow, gravel-bottomed bend in the river. The bend had been eroded by the current over decades until it had turned almost into a separate lake. Here a quiet boat could drift across the shallow gravel and easily spot here and there the long, dark, menacing outlines of the torpedo-like pike as they drifted in and out of the reed beds or hung motionless in more open water.

Martin and his friend drifted over the place keeping low in the boat and on their first drift they spotted more than a dozen massive pike. This was strange enough in itself. One or two large pike might often be seen close together, but not a dozen or more – and these were big, strong river pike accustomed to hunting down fast-swimming fish that used the current out in the broad river to try to make good their escape.

Martin and his friend anchored their boat a little to the side of the great bow in the river, but the position of the sun and the bright golden gravel of the bottom of the river meant they could still see the pike and indeed their own baits. Martin decided to use a dace that he had caught that morning. He cast it well above the biggest pike he could see – it was undoubtedly one of the 20-pounders (9.1kg) and its head was just visible at the end of a weed bed.

Gradually, while keeping an eye both on the pike and on the dace, Martin worked his bait down towards the big pike. This was a technique he'd adopted on countless previous occasions and it almost never failed. The dace was inched toward the pike which, judging by its appearance, had no inkling that anything was amiss. But then when the dace was right in front of the pike it was as if the giant fish had been scalded. It reversed nervously into the weed bed and then bolted back out into the main river. Most extraordinary of all, all the other pike bolted as well. Martin and his friend were astonished. The pike could not have seen them or their tackle before the bait appeared in front of the fish's nose and once the dead dace had been seen by the pike it would normally have been snaffled up in a second. It was possible, thought Martin, that the pike had been hooked on a dace before, but the river was rarely if ever fished for pike so it seemed unlikely. And why did all the pike bolt at the same time? That too was unheard of. Martin and his friend waited an hour or so until they noticed that, almost imperceptibly, the pike had returned to the wide sluggish bend in the river.

Over the next couple of days Martin tried using small jack pike to tempt the big ones in the river; he tried roach and herring strips; he tried spinners and plugs. Nothing would entice any of the pike and as soon as one rushed away in terror the whole gang of them did the same. Throughout his long fishing life Martin had never come across anything like this and he was never to come across it again. Whatever he tried, the pike team were having none of it and Martin at least was convinced that they had, in some inexplicable way, been helping each other.

HIGHLY UNLIKELY

SCOTLAND, 1900

Fishermen are supposed to be terrible liars. If they lose a fish they always claim it was a huge one; if a fish breaks their line, it must have been a record-breaker. But fishing being a curious, some would say eccentric, pursuit, some lies turn out not to be quite such untruths after all.

A party of anglers from England were on holiday in a remote Scottish hotel. Every day they fished Loch Rannoch. There were four in the party and they fished two to a boat, each boat being rowed by a gillie. On their first days out on the loch they caught plenty of small fish – perhaps three or four to the pound (0.45kg). They fished a drift along the same shore, but well away from each other. When evening came on, the two boats rowed for the boathouse and though one was well behind the other the occupants were able to wave to each other. They had to pass through a narrow channel just a few hundred yards before they reached the boathouse and it was here in the narrowest channel that one of the two fishermen in the second boat claimed, later on, that he'd risen a massive trout. The gillie said nothing. This was a paying customer and he was canny enough to realise that he was not being paid to express his views about anything as contentious as this. Certainly he found the claim odd as he'd been rowing the boat and he'd seen nothing, but the fisherman had certainly been fishing as they came through the gap.

The fishermen in the first boat were scathing at dinner that night. 'You couldn't possibly have risen a trout of any kind let alone a really big one in that gap. The water's too shallow and we'd just rowed through it moments before. If anything had been there it would have bolted long before you even got within casting distance.'

Despite these remarks the fisherman who claimed he'd risen the fish stuck to his guns. He really had seen a massive trout turn over his fly whatever the others said.

Next day the two boats set off exactly as they had the day before. The weather was perfect for loch fishing – a stiff breeze, plenty of cloud cover, but the air balmy. Trout rose all over the lake and what they lacked in size they made up for in tenacity and fighting spirit.

When the two boats turned for home that second evening they were in high spirits. It had been a most enjoyable day, but when they got back to the hotel they were in for a shock.

The fisherman who'd claimed he'd risen a big trout as they returned to the boathouse had another story. This one was even more improbable than the first.

'I was in exactly the same place again as last evening when another massive trout rose, took my fly and was hooked. Unfortunately he was on for only a few moments, but he was a hell of a fish – over 10lb (4.5kg) if he weighed an ounce.'

Now the other fishermen had invited this chap on a whim. He was a friend of a friend and no one knew him really well. He'd seemed nice enough and was clearly a keen fisherman but if they'd known he was going to try to get away with these outrageous lies they never would have invited him in the first place.

That evening dinner was a sombre affair. Somehow this interloper who simply didn't play by the rules had spoilt the fun of their two days. It was bad enough to try to get away with a very unlikely tale on day one, but to pretend that the same thing had happened in the same place and at the same time the next day was just going too far. Thank heavens, they thought to themselves, tomorrow is our last day.

Another perfect day saw the same two boats on the loch. Fewer fish rose, but those that were caught were much bigger. One boat landed a fish over the magic 1lb (0.45kg) mark. The other boat had half a dozen small fish and a beauty of nearly 2lb (0.9kg).

Evening came and once again the two boats turned for home. Boat number one slipped through the narrow gap on the way to the boathouse, followed a few moments later by boat number two. The fisherman responsible for the tall stories of earlier days was in his usual position at the back of the second boat and as ever he continued to cast as they rowed slowly along. As they reached the narrowest part of the channel – just the place where he'd claimed to have risen a huge fish and then, on the following day, hooked one – just as he reached the same spot a massive boil showed 30ft (9.1m) behind the second boat and the fight was on.

The gillie slowed the boat to a standstill. The fisherman in the back of the boat played his fish as if his life depended on it. Line tore off the reel as the fish shot away from the narrows and back towards deeper water. At the boathouse the first boat had been stowed and its occupants were on their way to the hotel oblivious to the events taking place back on the lake.

Meanwhile the gillie waited anxiously with his net while the fisherman kept his rod up and stayed in touch with a fish that was now more than 100 yards (91.4m) away. The fisherman in the bow of the boat sat with his mouth open, speechless.

Gradually the great fish began to tire and a few minutes later a wild, beautifully marked 11lb (5kg) brown trout was swung aboard in the gillie's net.

When the fisherman arrived back at the hotel the proprietor insisted that the fish should be laid on a great dish in the hall for all to see. But it wasn't until they came down to dinner an hour later that the fisherman's two companions from the first boat saw the great fish. They stopped, they started and they declared at precisely the same moment that they simply didn't believe what their eyes were telling them.

Without being told they immediately knew that this fish must have been caught by their friend; by the man they had judged a liar. Somehow they also knew that he had caught the fish exactly where he'd said he'd risen and then hooked those earlier giants.

The two fishermen sought out their friend, apologised for ever doubting him and congratulated him on a magnificent effort. The successful fisherman, modest to the last, merely replied:

'I think I was rather lucky. Probably tired him out when I hooked him the previous night!'

OFFICIAL RECORD

ENGLAND, 1901

It had been a pretty miserable fishing career by any standards. He'd once been taken fishing by a friend from his office in the City. First cast with a borrowed rod and reel he'd hooked a beautiful, wild, 3lb (1.4kg) brown trout. It was the best fish that had been taken from that bit of river in more than a decade. In the clubhouse that evening he'd been applauded, his health drunk several times over dinner. He had never felt so elated before in his life. It was like the thrill he'd felt the day he had learned to ride his bicycle unaided as a child.

Two days after that first outing he had to visit his tailor and it was then that he realised fate was taking a hand in all this because two doors along from his tailor was one of London's oldest and most exclusive fishing tackle dealers. He'd never even noticed the shop before. Like a man in a trance he walked through the shop door and emerged two hours later with three rods, three reels, a beautiful tackle bag, several boxes of flies, lines, casts, net and all the other essential requirements for the enthusiastic fisherman. He joined the best syndicate on an exclusive stretch of the best chalkstream in the south of England and fished every weekend throughout the season. When he took his annual holiday he took it on the river and fished every day.

It was amazing how that initial fish was able to inspire an enthusiasm that carried its victim – if victim he was

– through more than a decade of bad luck, for try as he might the fisherman could never repeat the success of that first glorious day. He caught many fish it is true, but they were always small and always caught rather messily and by accident. He watched enviously as other anglers wandered the banks, caught sight of a rising fish, cast to it, hooked it and landed it. The smooth, beautifully efficient nature of their strategy and skill was almost more than he could bear. Despite his superb tackle and numerous lessons with expert casters he could never throw a line like his fellow club members. If he spotted a rising fish his cast was always hurried and bungled. He put the fish down and then perhaps didn't see another all day. All around him other fishermen saw fish he couldn't see and caught them, but despite the endless misery of his lack of ability the fisherman would not give up. The memory of that first fish was too strong and he was determined to recapture that early rapture. Then

everything changed. The fisherman arrived at the river on a morning that at first seemed like a thousand others that had failed to live up to his expectations. It was a mild day in May with a light breeze and though he experienced a general sense of well-being as he set off along the bank there was nothing to indicate that this was going to be a very special day indeed.

He cast and rose a beautiful trout of nearly 2lb (0.9kg). His heart soared. Perhaps he was about to enjoy the luck for which he'd waited so long. Next cast came another fish, then another. Each beautifully marked brown trout weighed well over 1lb (0.45kg). By noon he had reached the legally allowed limit for the river. But how could he stop? This was the day when everything was at last falling into place. He had to make a decision. Stop fishing immediately – which he was obliged by the law and the rules of the club to do – or carry on fishing in the knowledge that if he was caught he would be up before the magistrate and fined. He would almost certainly also be thrown out of the club. What should he do? He decided that after waiting so long for a truly great day he would risk everything. If he packed up he might never again have such luck.

The afternoon wore on and his luck held. By five o'clock he had caught 16 more fish than he was supposed to take in one day. It had been worth the risk but he decided it was time to make a dash for it while the going was good. The keeper was due to make his rounds at six and he would need to be off the water well before that to make sure there was no chance of bumping into the man.

He reached the roadway and was looking forward to getting home and contacting the local taxidermist. Despite the cost he had a mind to have every last fish mounted in memory of the greatest day's fishing he had enjoyed or was ever likely to enjoy. The fish would be proof for all his friends that he really could catch fish. Until now they simply assumed he was an incompetent angler, something that had long rankled in his mind. Now he would show them. He stepped up on to the roadway and walked straight into a policeman. They exchanged pleasantries but there was clearly something odd about the angler's nervous demeanour. The policeman became suspicious. He kept looking down at the angler's wicker creel, which groaned under the weight of the fish it contained.

'We've had a lot of poaching along here of late,' said the policeman.

'I can well believe it,' said the angler, who was now sweating with fear. He put his basket down and wiped his brow and before he could do anything about it the policeman had stooped down and flipped the lid of the creel open. Why on earth had he forgotten to do up the leather straps?

The policeman looked up.

'I think you'd better come with me,' he said. The fish were confiscated and the poor angler charged with taking fish illegally. He was told he must present himself in the local magistrates' court in two weeks' time. Disgraced and certain to lose his club membership, the fisherman had also forfeited his tackle. As he took the train home he felt he wanted to die. The worst thing was not the loss of his tackle; not the loss of his club membership or the fine that the magistrate was bound to impose. No, the worst part of the whole thing was having lost the fish: he would never now be able to prove to his friends that he had indeed caught such a magnificent bag. Then he had a brainwave. It was an idea that might just save the day.

When he appeared in the magistrates' court two weeks later he was given a severe telling off. The magistrate read out the charge and asked the clerk of the court to make an official record that the angler before them had been caught in possession of 26 brown trout with an average weight of nearly 2lb (0.9kg). 'This is not the sort of behaviour we would expect from a responsible adult,' said the magistrate.

'Now, do you have anything to say for yourself?'

It was at that moment that the angler spoke up. 'Yes,' he said. 'Can I have a certified copy of the court records to show my friends?' The magistrate was furious at this frivolous request. Apart from fining him five shillings for the fishing offence there was nothing he could do. The fisherman was perfectly entitled to a record of the proceedings. He was duly given his copy of the court record and he went away with a smile on his face. He had the court record expensively framed and hung it above the fireplace in his sitting room. When he died he stipulated in his will that his son would not be entitled to any of his money if he disposed of the framed court record.

GILLIE GETS ONE

SCOTLAND, 1901

There is a story told of a Scottish gillie who took a man out to fish the Pass of Brander near where the main road runs along the river from Dalmally to Oban. The road sticks close to the water's edge on the north side and it was from this bank that an angler was fishing one day during the last year of Queen Victoria's reign.

The pool upon which his efforts were directed was the one known as the Brander, a slow-flowing pool, situated just where the water leaves the loch. Late on in the afternoon, not having had any sport, he relinquished his rod and went for a short walk. No sooner had the fisherman gone than a brilliant idea flashed through his gillie's mind – why shouldn't he try a cast from the opposite bank? He had no right to fish from the opposite bank, but he had a boat and a strong feeling that he might well get a fish. The far bank would let him cast into a deep glide that always held a few of the very big fish that occasionally came up the river. He rowed to the opposite bank, tied up the boat, and moving gradually up the stream started to fish.

A hundred yards or so from the place where he'd left the boat the gillie hooked a massive fish. Its first great rush almost stripped the spool of the reel down to the bare metal, but the gillie was a skilled fisherman who knew just what his tackle could do and putting as much pressure as he dared on the rod he just held the fish. At that moment the gillie's client returned from his walk. The gentleman was not in the least happy to see his gillie away over on the far bank into what was clearly a very large fish. In fact he became so cross that he shouted across to the gillie to cut the line. The gillie refused and suggested that the gentleman should return to the hotel since it was now evening and tell one of the other boatmen that he was into a big fish and needed help. The fisherman mumbled and grumbled and complained that he was being shabbily treated but he eventually did as he was asked and set off for the hotel.

The gillie continued to play the fish which, instead of tiring, seemed to grow ever more powerful and unpredictable. The gillie's last words to the departing fisherman were that he did not intend to part with that salmon before he was absolutely obliged. And once again he asked that the angler, on arriving at the hotel, should without fail tell one of the boatmen of the awkward position in which the gillie found himself. The gillie especially asked that the boatman should be told that this was a very big fish indeed, perhaps the biggest ever from the river which had many times in the past produced salmon of over 40lb (18.1kg). The gillie was an experienced man and in his heart believed that this fish might well weigh more than 60lb (27.2kg). He had never felt anything like it before.

The angler promptly followed the first part of the gillie's advice. Perhaps he was a good deal annoyed at his gillie's conduct and thought that he had had no right to fish from the farther side; or perhaps he thought he would administer a salutary lesson to a man who hooked a giant salmon for himself rather than for his client. Whatever the reason, one thing is certain; he calmly returned to the hotel and had dinner, and in due course went to bed, and omitted to mention to anyone what had become of his gillie.

Thus the hours went by and the unhappy gillie still held on pluckily to the great fish. Futilely he hoped that each moment would bring help. The darkness of the night deepened; the fish kept up its deep and dogged patrol. The gillie was not a patient man but he was very determined and as the slow night wore on and the dawn came, each succeeding hour only added to his smouldering wrath. At last, between six and seven in the morning, he gave up all hope and, his muscles almost rigid with pain, he broke the tackle and returned home.

It was certainly a triumph for the salmon, which was no doubt a heavy fish. Indeed its weight increased in the telling, during the ensuing days, until it became of a fabulous size. It is easy to imagine the withering contempt felt by the valiant gillie for the angler who had left him in the lurch in such an unsportsmanlike fashion. There was little wonder that the unlucky gentleman had speedily to leave the hotel without ever showing his face again in the dining room or the bar. Indeed, despite the fact that he was a well-known, well-connected and very wealthy angler he knew that his behaviour had been beyond the pale and he never again returned to the hotel.

EPIC BATTLE

SCOTLAND, 1905

Loch Poulary is a picturesque stretch of water – a widening of the river, 1 mile (1.6km) long by a quarter of a mile (400m) wide , it has a woody promontory running out into it from a steep hillside on the south. Stretching away to the west, at the head, may be seen the dead-water of the river, leading the eye upward to one of the many surrounding rugged hills.

On the day of one of the most monumental battles ever known between man and salmon, the rain had raised the level of the loch nearly 3ft (0.9m), but it would fish all the better for that, for the weeds that in some places cause annoyance were well submerged. The gillie rowed steadily up the loch. The fisherman put his favourite rod together, a Hardy light split-cane trout rod, and selected a cast of flies that had a fair-sized Red-and-Teal on the tail.

The clouds had lifted from the lake by the time they had rowed into position, although the mountains were still mist-covered. Despite favourable appearances, the trout did not rise with the frequency one might have expected. Perhaps they had had too many good things to eat, of late.

Those that did come, however, were above the average size and meant business. They hooked themselves with absolute certainty. Towards the centre of the loch, near to the wooded promontory, was a shallow bank 30 yards (27.4m) long, generally known as the sunken island; a favourite place for both salmon and large trout to lie. As they approached the spot, the fisherman remarked to his gillie that the water looked favourable for the chance of a salmon. The gillie suggested that perhaps it might be worthwhile to put on a heavier-gut cast but with the same Red-and-Teal, for salmon are partial to that fly. To his eternal regret the fisherman ignored the advice and carried on using the cast he'd been using every day for a week. It was frayed and worn but would do, he thought.

There still lurked in the fisherman's mind a strong feeling that he would raise a salmon, which caused him to fish with extra care and attention. And sure enough before they had reached the end of the sunken island, up he came.

'He's on!' cried the gillie, but by then the fisherman didn't need telling. Only a very large fish could have made that slow, sullen disturbance of the water, which left the impression on the mind's eye of a glimpse of purple and silver. No distinct form of the fish was seen, only a dark wedge-shaped object for a second above the grey surface of the water – it was the upper half of a massive tail. With commendable presence of mind the fisherman waited until the swirl had vanished and then lifted his rod sharply.

Immediately the fisherman sensed that this was no ordinary fish. He was later to say that it seemed more as if boat, gillie and fisherman were hooked to the salmon than the other way around. It seemed as if they were being towed about at the sweet will of the huge creature. As he swam away he seemed oblivious of the fact that a dangerous hook was attached to his mouth, but how long would that last? What would be his next move? Such questions as these lashed the fisherman's mind as, with knees playing like castanets, he held on with hopeless determination to the alarmingly bucking trout rod.

The same trout rod had already in the earlier part of the week landed three salmon: two on Loch Poulary, the largest of which weighed 18½lb (8.4kg); but that fact was not calculated to inspire confidence, for the gut used for that earlier encounter had been much more powerful, and the rod – made from beautiful Tonkin cane – had almost certainly been weakened by such strenuous efforts. In the meantime, at any rate, the fish was behaving in a gentlemanly and sober manner, which allowed the decks to be cleared for action – it also allowed the fisherman to recover some of the composure necessary in such an emergency.

With bated breath he discussed tactics with the gillie and the probable conduct of affairs that the salmon might choose. It was then half past six, and under ordinary circumstances they would have had the fish in the boat and be home within the hour. But how much time would pass before they could conquer this sullen monster, taking his lordly way around the boat?

For 20 minutes the fisherman stared steadily, with eyes that ached and became dimmed with mist, at the point where the line, like a thin bar of steel, majestically cut its way through the water. Meanwhile the gillie rowed after the fish in a stately procession round the loch, always watching for a visible sign of the sudden change in tactics which he well knew the huge creature would sooner or later adopt.

In the end the gillie failed to notice the sudden change in the salmon's behaviour, but the fisherman felt it along the rod and down through the line. As time wore on, the fisherman became braver or perhaps more foolhardy. He began to exert a more powerful pressure on the unseen leviathan – until the small rod was well-nigh bent double, and then it was that the enemy seemed to awake to the understanding that some mysterious force was attempting to coerce him.

What he actually did in the depths below no one could tell; but the fisherman knew something had changed through a series of what felt like electric shocks passing up the line. Undoubtedly the fish was fast losing his temper; perhaps savagely shaking his hoary head and muttering smothered fish-curses at the dogged and pertinacious little creature that continued to tug at his jaw. Whatever the cause of these electric shocks, the fisherman fully realised that they were the forerunners of something more violent. Hardly had he begun to think this than the salmon made a terrific run, taking out fully 80 yards (73.2m) of line at lightning speed and finished off the demonstration by hurling itself sideways clean out of the water. The fisherman gasped at the huge size of the fish and the massive splash it made on re-entry. Luckily he had the sense to drop the point of his rod as the fish jumped or it surely would have been lost then and there.

At this point a non-fisherman might have said, 'Well, if he was running why didn't you stop him?' That is all very well, but it would have been as easy to stop a charging bull with a length of cotton thread.

The gillie, having seen the fish, was cursing their luck. How could they have attached themselves to this unbeatable creature?

'Why, the 18-pounder [8.2kg] the other day, when he jumped, looked a mere baby by the side of this one,' he said. 'He must be 40 or 50lb [18.1–22.7kg], surely?'

The fisherman was too shocked to reply.

After the jump there was a split second during which it really did seem as if the fish had thrown the hook, but then the line tightened again; the fish was still on. The 80 yards of line had been taken off the reel in one great rush lasting just a few seconds, but the fisherman could only regain the line slowly, inch by inch. It was like a tug of war; a grim contest between man and fish for every scrap of line. Then without warning they found they had rowed to within a few feet of the salmon. Looking down they could see its huge shape beneath them. A more dogged battle began with the fish lying deep and taking the boat once again on its slow procession round the loch. What was to be done? How the fisherman wished now that he had changed the cast.

It was long past the hour at which they were expected back at the hotel for dinner, but they were no nearer defeating the fish than they had been when they had first hooked it more than two hours earlier. And now the fish had begun to sulk. But what angler would think of dinner with a 40lb (18.1kg) salmon attached to the end of his line? All that could be done to rouse the monster was done. And in the end the simple expedient of slapping the extremity of the butt of the rod with a small stone was successful. The jarring had the desired effect and away he went again to the accompaniment of the raucous shrieking of the reel.

Would he never stop? There were only 120 yards (110m) of line altogether on the reel, but on, on he went, and smaller and smaller, and thinner and thinner became that coil of silk upon the drum of the reel. At last the fatal moment arrived; the last yard (91.4cm) of line was run out. The fisherman pointed the rod at the fish, and stretched out his arm to the utmost, with the vague idea of gaining another yard or so. There was one fierce pull, and for an instant the water boiled in the far distance, and then the sickening slackening of the line.

The fisherman looked at the gillie. The gillie stared at the fisherman. Neither spoke. Seconds passed without a word as the fisherman slowly wound up the loose line. Fortunately the gillie still said nothing. If he had spoken the fisherman might well have burst into tears.

But what was this? The line was beginning to tighten up again. 'By God, he's on, he's on still!' the fisherman shouted. And so he was. The sudden strain at the end of such a long rush had stopped the fish and turned him back.

It is the uncertainty of the thing that lends such charm to angling; the play upon the emotions. Here had the fisherman been a moment before in the depths of despair, and in a complete reversal his spirits soared. Convinced that the battle had been lost he suddenly found that he had been given another chance and against all the odds.

The sheer unexpected horrendous difficulty of the thing was what made fishing unlike any other sport or pastime. Even success in too large a dose could spoil it. The balance between success and failure was the thing that made it so addictive.

Our intrepid salmon fisherman himself remembered once catching over 200 trout on a very prolific day, but he'd grown bored with it and never wanted to do as well again.

But this giant salmon was another customer altogether.

With feverish haste he wound in the slack, trying to keep pace with the fish, which was now running at furious speed towards the boat. Again, as at the end of the first rush, the fish hurled himself bodily out of water; but this time he nearly terminated his career for good by flinging himself into the boat. He missed the bow by little more than a yard (91.4cm) and plunged on, jagging from side to side and boring ever deeper. But the uncanny beast was not even yet at the end of his resources; for he turned suddenly and once again made a tremendous run. This time he played what the fisherman later described as a devilish, mean and wily trick.

The reel was hoarsely screaming while the fisherman gazed eagerly in the direction in which the fish had started, but seconds later he heard a swish and a plunge behind his back. He turned in an instant and was just in time to see the monster throw itself out of water on the farther side of the boat. In other words, having set off on a 100-yard (91.4m) dash out in front of the boat the salmon had doubled back after 50 yards (45.7m) and retraced his swim exactly. This had the effect of pulling the thick silk main line into a vast bow, out in front of the boat and then back again, and all under water where the maximum pressure of drag would obtain.

For a moment the fisherman was so confused that he assumed the jumping fish behind him was a completely different salmon; but no, it was the old enemy that had taken a circle under the water, and was now once more displaying its singular agility.

At last the struggle, the endless wear and tear, was too much for the worn and harassed tackle to stand. The line, in a complete bow, had to pull against the whole weight of the enclosed water and the gut gave way.

For years afterwards the fisherman wondered what became of that huge salmon. He never again hooked anything as big, as clever or as tenacious and in his heart he sometimes thought that he was glad not to have ended such a noble life.

Perhaps the great fish fell a victim to the nets, when no amount of strength could save him; perhaps he returned again and again unmolested to his home river to pass on his extraordinary characteristics to countless future generations of salmon. Whatever had happened to him it was difficult not to take off one's hat to such an accomplished adversary.

When the fisherman examined his cast after the great salmon had gone he found that the Red-and-Teal fly had snapped off at the neck. Who knows but if the cast had been changed there might have been a different tale to tell, ending in glory, with the gillie playing the pipes until morning. As it was, the two men made their way dourly back to the hotel in the dark of early morning, while behind them, from a rift in the western sky, a deep red glow was shed over the landscape.

THE WAITING ROOM
ENGLAND, 1906

J.H.R. Bazeley was such an enthusiastic fisherman that he made the maximum use of a railway network that, by the end of the nineteenth century, had expanded to serve almost every region of Britain. In those far-off halcyon days before the Beeching cuts of the 1960s, trains stopped regularly throughout the day at remote villages where wonderful fishing was still to be had for a few shillings a day and sometimes even for nothing.

Bazeley was so fond of trains that he often left his fishing gear in railway station cloakrooms if that was more convenient than to carry it all back to his hotel in the evening.

Once he left rod, basket and bait (in the form of a large number of wasp grubs) in a great heap at a station in Swaledale, meaning to return in the morning and collect it all before catching the London train. But back at the hotel he received an urgent telegram and was forced to return to London that night leaving his tackle stranded.

Two weeks later a polite letter arrived from the stationmaster reminding Bazeley that his tackle was still sitting in that cloakroom in Swaledale. The stationmaster had spotted Bazeley's address on the brass plate on the top of his basket. But there was a warning. If the tackle basket was not collected within seven days it would be opened, the contents broken up and sold at auction to cover the cost of storage.

When Bazeley finally returned to Yorkshire – just in time to meet the deadline – he rushed into the cloakroom in time to see the attendant leap from a high stool while taking a swipe with a newspaper at a huge wasp. Bazeley noticed two or three other wasps circling dangerously overhead.

As soon as the attendant took possession of Bazeley's cloakroom ticket he shouted: 'A damned nice thing you've done! Making a convenience of the company for housing bees!'

The attendant was so incensed that Bazeley had to listen to him ranting and raving for more than ten minutes and all the while he leapt hither and thither swatting wildly in every direction.

'I'll not get your property. I'll not go near it. No one's been able to go near it for days – three staff are off sick after being stung. That corner's been like a musical box all week.' And with that he set off in pursuit of another menacing dive-bomber. 'No, I'll not get them for you. If you want your bloomin' bees you come and fetch them!' Bazeley dashed into the corner, lifted his basket and then ran out and round the corner to a shop where he could buy a large sheet of brown paper. He wrapped his basket securely and set off for home, his whole person appearing to buzz and rattle continually. Passers-by looked oddly at him; one or two even ran away when the parcel appeared not only to sing and hum but also to move.

At home he threw the wrapped basket into a large box and then introduced methylated spirits and sulphur to kill all the remaining wasps. By a miracle he wasn't stung once in the process.

For months afterwards every time Bazeley left his fishing tackle at the station it was looked upon with extreme suspicion by the people in charge and he was always asked the same question: 'Onny bees in 'ere, mister?'

WRONG SALMON

ENGLAND, 1908

Two Oxford academics were fishing the Northumberland Coquet for salmon on a freezing day in March. They would have been the first to admit that their technique left much to be desired, but their slightly ham-fisted casts were made worse by their uncontrollable shaking. The shaking was the result not so much of the cold as of the lack of clothing. The two were famously forgetful.

Towards lunchtime one of the two was trailing his fly in the water some way downstream while he tried to unknot a tangle at the reel end. Just as he straightened the line he noticed that it had started to fly through his hands. Hardly believing his luck he lifted his rod and was into a good salmon. After playing the fish for five minutes he felt warmer than he had all day and he was only hampered by his friend who, terrified that he might not be in the right position with the net when the fish finally gave up, was constantly getting in the way. But the hook hold was a good one, the tackle was strong and the fish definitely seemed to be tiring.

The man with the net had waded into the water by now to be closer to the fish when the time came. Then without warning he saw a white flash in the water, lunged at it with his net and – somewhat to his surprise – landed the fish.

'We've done it!' he shouted.

'What on earth are you talking about?' said his friend.

'The fish is nowhere near you. It's tiring but it's still in the middle of the river.'

It was then that the man with the net realised that by some extraordinary chance he had accidentally netted a salmon that had simply been swimming by.

But it was just as well for minutes later the fish that really had been hooked got the line round an underwater obstruction and in an instant was gone.

History does not record how long it took for the two hapless academics to confess just how lucky they had been to bag a 15lb (6.8kg) salmon once they had returned to Oxford.

BRANDY AS A
FISH REVIVER

ENGLAND, 1910

Edgar Stanhope, an Oxford scientist who also happened to be a keen angler, carried out a number of experiments using brandy as a means of restoring life to dying fish.

Having kept a trout out of water until it had apparently died he would then drop it into a bucket filled with undiluted brandy. On the first occasion he tried this he commented:

'It was highly interesting to see the plucky manner a trout battled with his fainting condition, after a dose of brandy, and came out the conqueror.'

On his next visit to the Wye, Dr Stanhope took his bucket of brandy out in the boat – to the amusement of the local gillies – and tried the same experiment with a salmon. The results were less impressive, as Stanhope himself admitted:

'Strange to say, the salmon did not once attempt to rouse himself after being dosed, the consequence being fatal to him. This was the only fish that succumbed under the treatment.'

Stanhope then tried the experiment with a few coarse fish. He was most impressed by the effect of brandy on the dace:

'I had him out of the water three times of five minutes each. He was exceedingly faint and almost dead, but immediately the brandy was given he pulled himself together and in the course of a few minutes not only recovered, but darted around with a rapidity positively amazing.'

CHEEKY CARP
ENGLAND, 1910

Arthur Ransome, best known for children's stories like *Swallows and Amazons,* is probably the only really stylish angling writer of the twentieth century. His book *Rod and Line* has little in it that will help you catch more or bigger fish, but Ransome can be relied on to get right to the heart of what makes fishing so appealing and he usually does it by describing nothing more than a day catching gudgeon, or watching the anglers on some remote Russian river ply their rods.

Ransome was himself a very keen angler, though disarmingly modest about his abilities.

Only once did he land a carp and it was an experience so shattering that he wrote about it at length. Catching just one carp may sound like a pretty poor show, but until modern tackle and techniques began to develop in the 1950s, carp were considered almost uncatchable. They were seen as huge, mysterious fish, the inscrutable inhabitants of deep, long-forgotten lakes. They would rarely take a bait and if by chance one was hooked its speed, power and cunning almost always meant the fisherman's tackle was smashed before he realised what had hit him.

Ransome said that even the salmon could not match the carp's appalling pace and anyone who has caught both would probably agree with him.

The difficulties of catching carp when Ransome was writing in the early 1900s can be judged by the fact that the British record stood at about 20lb (9.1kg) at that time. Carp commonly grow to twice that size or more.

When Ransome hooked his carp he was using a multiplier and rod combination on which he'd caught numerous large salmon. Yet when he hooked his carp with the same tackle he admitted he simply could not keep in touch with it. More by luck than judgement he managed to land the fish and was astonished to discover, after what he considered an epic battle, that it was really quite a small specimen.

On that same day Ransome had a bizarre and quite unforgettable encounter with another carp. He hooked the fish late in the afternoon and realised immediately that fish rather than angler was in control of events. As soon as it was hooked the carp set off at a blistering pace for the far side of the lake. It was so quick that Ransome could not give it line in time and the cast snapped like cotton. Then there occurred one of the strangest events of Ransome's long angling career.

His line had snapped 12in (30.5cm) or so above his float and while considering how or even whether he should tackle up again he kept an eye on the lost float, which lay flat on the water and still well out towards the middle of the pond. As he watched, he saw the float begin to move. It sailed directly towards Ransome's feet. When it came to within 6ft (1.8m) of the edge of the lake the float stopped, there was a mighty swirl and a great bronze flank was seen to shoot off towards deeper water. Using his net Ransome retrieved his float, which still had its hook and weights attached.

As he remarked later, it was as though the fish had returned his tackle as if to say: 'Not a bad first attempt. Do try again.'

UP THE FALLS

SCOTLAND, 1910

Erosion and man-made changes – weirs, hydroelectric systems and dams – can destroy a salmon river in a matter of months. Occasionally a man-made change to a river can have the reverse effect and help restore it as a fishery, but the situation that existed at one time on the River Orrin in Easter Ross must be unique.

The river had once boasted a healthy run of salmon, but the fish had to leap up a waterfall that, after centuries of erosion, eventually reached a height of nearly 14ft (4.3m).

Now salmon can get up falls of much greater height but only if they can leap in stages. If the fall of water is heavy enough they will land in the full flood halfway up and swim there for a few seconds before leaping the second stage. But on the Orrin the falls were sheer with an overhang, so the 13½ft (4.1m) perhaps 14ft (14.3m) had to be cleared in one leap.

Many people watched the salmon attempt the jump, but it was rare – and quite extraordinary – to see a fish make it to the top.

In earlier times a barrier had been built halfway up the falls to help the fish over. Somehow the barrier had been broken or worn away and the salmon, or the vast majority of them anyway, could only mill around in the pool below the falls. An old gillie known as Macdonald who lived in a cottage so remote that it was sometimes cut off in winter for months at a time, remembered a time when the local landowner, feeling sorry for the poor old salmon leaping again and again but quite ineffectually, would stand at the edge of the falls for hour after hour with a large landing net in his hands. As a salmon leapt perhaps 8–10ft (2.4–3m) in the air he would catch it in the net in mid-air and carry it up to the upper reach of the river where it was gently released. On some days he netted and moved fish like this for hours at a time until in fact he was almost exhausted.

DUFFER'S DELIGHT

ENGLAND, 1911

Mayfly time on southern English chalkstreams has always
been known as Duffer's Fortnight. The reason is not hard
to fathom – for a few short days, a week or two at the very
most, the mayfly hatch can turn otherwise wily trout into
suicidal maniacs that will rise to anything and everything.
Anglers have been known to take fish on little bits of white
cloth, on old bedraggled flies that resemble nothing in
particular, even on bare hooks.

Trout enjoying a frenzied feeding spree can take lemming-
like behaviour to ridiculous extremes.

An angler fishing a very famous stretch of the Test at mayfly
time was having a field day. He'd caught so many fish after
just two hours' fishing that he decided to pack up. But like
so many anglers in a similar position he couldn't resist one
last cast. He'd seen what he thought was a particularly big
trout rising continually under the far bank and he decided
to try for it. Now this fisherman was a bit of a rogue and
as an experiment he decided to try something not illegal
at this time, but definitely a little unsporting when the
fish were so easy to catch anyway. The fisherman set up a
North Country wet-fly cast – in other words, a cast with a
point fly and two droppers. The fisherman tied a traditional
Mayfly pattern on the end of the cast and two very odd-
looking home-made flies to the droppers. One of these flies
was made from an old piece of carpet fibre. It was bright

red, very bushy and completely unlike anything any self-respecting chalkstream trout could ever have seen before. The same was true of the other fly, which the fisherman had tied to imitate a water beetle. It was big and black and hairy and about 1in (2.5cm) long and ½in (1.3cm) wide.

Having set up his cast and checked to see that no one was coming, our intrepid fisherman performed a perfect cast. His line sailed out across the river and landed like thistledown – on the other bank! Often when this happens the skilful angler will gently ease the line back towards him and it will, against all expectation, not get hooked up on the bankside vegetation. Instead it drops perfectly on to the water and over the waiting fish. That's what often happens if one fly is involved but our cheating fisherman was pushing his luck with three hooks. He tried as delicately as possible to draw his line back. The first dropper fell into the water; then the second, but the point fly caught on a stump.

The fisherman tried a strong pull, a sideways yank, a gentle waggle. Nothing would dislodge his fly from the stump. He decided that rather than damage his rod by constant pulling he would pull for a break using his hands. There was no alternative. The fisherman put his rod gently on the bank and grabbed the line. For just a few seconds this meant that, over on the far bank, the point fly was trapped on the stump but the rest of the cast stretched out over the water. The two droppers dangled enticingly on the water. The line grew tighter as the fisherman on the opposite bank pulled harder and harder. Then in a flash the fisherman saw not one, but two trout come up and take the droppers. The cast plunged into the water and the astonished fisherman dropped the line and picked up his rod hoping that there might be a chance of landing at least one of the trout. The rod bucked and kicked as the two trout struggled in different directions and it was a moment or two before the fisherman realised that their struggles had freed the point fly – the Mayfly pattern – from the stump. With two fish on, this was a battle the fisherman was likely to lose, but he was using much stronger gut than he would normally at mayfly time and he was at least in with a chance.

One trout was netted safely and the fisherman was trying to manoeuvre the second fish into the net when he spotted out of the corner of his eye a third fish turning at the bedraggled point fly.

It was at this moment that the fisherman's luck deserted him. The third fish was much bigger than either of the others, and as it plunged towards the riverbed, it pulled the gut cast down and the line caught on the edge of the net and parted. The fisherman almost burst into tears. To have landed three fish on one cast and in such a unique way would have been the achievement of a lifetime.

Two days later the fisherman was back at the same spot on the river casting quite properly with a single Mayfly. He felt frustrated because he had been unable to tell his friends about his exceptional experience earlier the same week. But mayfly time was coming to an end and he thought he would at least enjoy one more day on the river before the fishing became very much more difficult indeed. Then he realised he had forgotten his amadou – a specially treated piece of fungus once carried by fishermen to dry out their flies each time they became waterlogged. This was awkward because within two or three casts the amadou was essential if the fisherman was to avoid having to change his fly.

It was too late to return home so the fisherman fished his fly until it sank and then carried on fishing anyway. Moments later he was reeling in when he hooked a fish. Delighted at finding success despite his forgetfulness, the fisherman knew exactly what his tackle could do and he soon had the fish within sight of the net – except it wasn't one fish. It was two! And neither fish had taken the fisherman's Mayfly. In a flash he realised that by a million-to-one chance he had hooked the line that still joined the two fish he'd lost two days earlier.

HELPING HAND
SCOTLAND, 1911

One of the great excitements of fishing is the first great rush that a fish makes after you've hooked it. It's exciting because it's so dangerous – more fish are probably lost in those few moments than at any other time. Hold the fish too hard during that initial rush and your line will break, fail to keep some sort of control and the fish will swim into a dense bed of weeds and snag you; let the line go slack and the hook may well fall out. If you survive this, your chances of landing the fish increase dramatically – assuming you recover from the fit of shaking induced by those first few moments of terror.

Very occasionally a fish that has weeded itself can still be brought to the bank but getting it out of the weeds is very difficult indeed. Anglers have been known to throw boulders in or even strip off and swim into the weeds in an attempt to move the fish on. In the heady days of Edwardian luxury when wealthy salmon fishers journeyed north each spring for the salmon fishing and when, according to some commentators, gentlemen really were still gentlemen, it was very much the done thing to help a fellow angler out whenever one could.

An elderly colonel fishing an obscure Scottish river hooked a salmon far bigger than anything that had ever been caught on that river before. The fish was such a good one in fact that the elderly colonel was terrified that he would lose it.

When the fish took his fly he simply assumed it was one of the 5–10-pounders (2.3–4.5kg) that were common in the river in the early part of the season. That meant a lost fish. It was only after the battle had settled into a steady pattern that the colonel realised that, for this river, this was indeed the fish of a lifetime, and he was determined not to lose it. Up and down the pool went the salmon, sedately but with a curious kind of unyielding heaviness.

After this had gone on for some time the salmon must have realised that something was seriously amiss. It panicked and shot downstream into the next pool. Luckily the colonel was able to follow, running frantically over the boulder-strewn bank with his rod held as high as he could manage. At the next pool the fish calmed down again, but to his horror the colonel saw that all along the bank in his new position was a great raft of weed stretching out 20ft (6.1m) into the river. No sooner had he seen the weed than the fish saw it too and vanished into the thickest part.

The colonel knew from the pressure on his line that the fish was well and truly embedded in the weed, which stretched a good 100 yards (91.4m) up- and downstream from his position. If he could have waded to the opposite bank any pressure exerted on the fish would have pulled it away from the weeds, but pull from his bank and every bit of pressure simply drove the fish further into the morass. The colonel knew he was beaten and he prepared to pull for a break. Just then an angler wandered by on the opposite bank. The old colonel shouted across and explained the situation and to his astonishment his fellow angler immediately said he thought he could help. The colonel watched bewildered as his fellow angler set up a salmon fly rod and tied on a large Hairy Mary. He then shouted to the colonel to keep the point of his rod up to ensure that the line to the salmon was tight. The colonel, still mystified, obeyed. Then the fisherman on the opposite bank began to cast. When 20 yards (18.3m) or so of line had been extended the old colonel thought the fly was going to land on his head or at least hit him in the face. But then he saw the Hairy Mary catch his line. As soon as that happened the angler on the opposite bank began to reel in furiously. The colonel's line was pulled towards the opposite bank, which, of course, had the effect of pulling the salmon out of the weeds. And after a few anxious moments that's exactly what happened. Keeping both the lines tight the two men then walked the salmon downstream until it was well past the raft of weed. Here the old colonel safely netted his fish. It weighed a little over 20lb (9.1kg). He shouted his thanks across the water and, having unhooked his fish, looked up again to ask his rescuer to come and have a drink at his hotel. But the other fisherman had gone. And the old colonel never saw him again.

COACHMAN
ENGLAND, 1912

No one alive today can remember when the horse and carriage was still a common means of getting about, but one or two centenarians still recall traps and gigs and broughams which didn't finally vanish, even from the streets of London, until the 1920s.

In more remote rural districts horse transport of one kind or another was widely used until the Second World War. One elderly fisherman remembered as a boy being taken fishing on the River Wye. He had never fished before, but his father set up the rod and advised the boy to start by worming. When he was a little older it would be time enough to learn to fly fish.

The little boy started to fish and, having no luck, gradually wandered away from his father. He reached a narrow bridge and thinking – as little boys always seem to think – that he would have more luck if he fished straight into the middle of the little river he decided that the bridge would be the perfect spot.

Having reached a point midway across the bridge he lowered his worm into the river. Seconds later his rod almost left his hand as a good fish took the bait and headed for the sea. The little boy had listened carefully when the art of fishing had been explained to him that morning and he remembered enough to give a running fish line. Having survived the first run, he realised that the fish was not so big after all and he really might land it. Two minutes later the little boy was trying to make up his mind whether to be delighted or disappointed at the big and decidedly slimy eel jumping around at his feet. Having tried several times to grab this impossible creature and each time come away with a handful of incredibly slippery slime he had almost decided to give up, leave everything where it was and fetch his father when the clatter of hooves caught his attention.

Seconds later a large and very stylish carriage appeared on the bridge and stopped. The snorting grey horses seemed enormous to the little boy. The carriage stayed put, the horses shuffled and blew, the boy stared and nothing happened. Then the carriage door opened, an elderly man stepped down out of the carriage and without saying a word opened his pocket knife, cut off the eel's head, extracted the boy's hook and handed it back to him. He then shook the little boy's hand, climbed back into his carriage and was gone.

KNOTTY PROBLEM

ENGLAND, 1913

For decades J. Arthur Hutton kept a detailed record of his
fishing on the Herefordshire Wye. Before the Great War the
Wye was still a great river with a good head of spring and
autumn salmon. It attracted anglers from far and wide and
produced some very big individual specimens. Hutton's
documentation of the last decades of the nineteenth
century and the first years of the twentieth provide a
unique account of a river that is now a pale shadow of its
former self. But his record also reveals some exceptional
days' fishing. Among the most startling was the occasion
on which he hooked a salmon estimated at well over 20lb
(9.1kg) in the Carrot's Pool. He played the fish for some
time and then, just for an instant, he was convinced he'd
lost the fish. Everything went slack, but no sooner had this
happened than everything tightened up again and the battle
recommenced.

But something had happened and this was a fish that
had doubled in strength. Hutton was astonished. He had
assumed that his fish was pretty nearly beaten, but now
it was as if it had never been hooked at all. The power of
each run was astonishing and nothing Hutton could do had
the least effect on this demon of a fish. At long last, and
more than an hour after he'd hooked the fish, an exhausted
Hutton finally discovered the secret of his salmon's
awesome strength and stamina. In that earlier moment

when he thought he'd lost the fish he really had lost it. The line had broken where it was tied to the hook, but by an extraordinary accident the end of the line had twisted itself into a loop and this loop, having run down the length of the fish, had managed to snare the salmon's tail. A fish hooked in the tail has its head, which explained the ferociousness of the ensuing battle.

ANOTHER NESSIE?

NORTH WALES, 1913

Lake Padarn in North Wales is deep, very deep. And in the deepest places can be found one of Britain's rarest fish – the char.

The char is a leftover from the last great Ice Age. When the ice sheets retreated the fish were left stranded only in the deepest lakes – Padarn and a few others in the Lake District – where temperatures could be relied on to plummet far enough to allow the fish to breed.

At one time, long lines with teams of bright flies were employed to catch the fish in numbers – almost, one might say, a commercial fishery – but the char have dwindled and now only the local anglers know where they might, just occasionally, still be caught.

A local man fishing just before the First World War caught six heavy char from a boat on Padarn. He was astonished. To catch one or two a week was usually good going. He was so excited he decided to head for home to tell his friends how well he had done, but first he would have one last cast. His flies were attached to a heavy weight and he felt it sink far down until it touched bottom.

Just then dark clouds appeared over the hills that ring the lake and the wind began to buffet his small boat. It looked like a storm was coming, and storms on Padarn can be dangerous when one has only a small rowing boat. He decided it was time to go. As he reeled in something snatched violently at his lures. The rod bucked and then arched violently towards the lake surface.

He had never hooked a fish that felt so strong. Each time he gained a few feet of line the fish quickly regained it, and gradually, as the great beast swam ever deeper, he saw the line diminishing on his reel. Soon all his line would be gone and with it the fish.

Endless minutes seemed to pass and the storm grew in intensity. Still the fish refused to tire. Fearing for his safety the fisherman decided he would give no more line, and besides he was only seconds away from the end of his line anyway. If his tackle broke so be it. He lifted the rod and the line tightened until the wind sang through it. At last, with a fearful crack, the line gave way and the fish was gone. The fisherman turned for home and just then he saw a large black back breach the waves, perhaps 100 yards (91.4m) in front of him. It was no char. It was at least 2ft (61cm) across the back, he later said, and seemed at least 6ft (1.8m), perhaps 8ft (2.4m) long, with a broad tail more like that of a whale than a fish. After breaching the 'fish' slowly sank out of sight. The fisherman reported what he had seen to the local newspaper and the strange creature was dubbed Padarn's own Nessie, after the Loch Ness monster. But what the great fish really was remains a mystery.

BULL BAITING

ENGLAND, 1915

The writer J.H.R. Bazeley fished all over Britain during the early years of the twentieth century, but he never felt quite as at home as he did when fishing his native Yorkshire. He was also unusual in fishing for both trout and coarse fish with equal pleasure at a time when trout fishers were often decidedly snooty about the coarse fishing fraternity.

Bazeley seems to have gone his own way in every respect and when disaster occurred he simply tried to make the best of it. He was once fishing a good grayling river and failed to notice – probably because he was wading at the time and had caught several good fish – that a large and very fierce bull had been watching him. By the time Bazeley, happily casting from his position midstream, noticed the bull he couldn't get back to his tackle. The bull was about 10ft (3m) away from a favourite fish basket, tackle bag and spare rod. Worse, the basket contained several very good grayling. Bazeley did not like the prospect of losing any of these things, but what was he to do?

Attack being the best form of defence, he decided to wade a little further downstream, quietly come ashore and then try to frighten the bull away. The first part of the plan succeeded. He reached the bank about 30 yards (27.4m) downstream of the bull, which still seemed intent on goings-on in the middle of the river. Bazeley found an old half-rotten piece of fence post and a couple of large clods of earth. He threw them at the bull while bellowing all kinds of dire threats. The bull turned, looked at Bazeley and charged. Bazeley beat a hasty retreat, but this time across a rickety wooden bridge by which he'd been standing. To Bazeley's astonishment the bull attempted to cross and only reversed off the footbridge when it began to sway violently under the bull's enormous weight. Outmanoeuvred, the bull let out a roar and trotted back to Bazeley's vulnerable-looking pile of tackle. Here, to Bazeley's lifelong astonishment, it began to do a sort of crazy war dance on top of rods, basket and box. In a few moments Bazeley's favourite gear was reduced to a crunched and broken pile of fragments. His fish had been mashed into the mud, his basket and box smashed beyond repair. His rod was in at least 15 pieces. Then, honour satisfied, the bull trotted off to a distant part of its field and left Bazeley to pick up the pieces and set off for home.

THE DARK FIGURE

ENGLAND, 1916

J.H.R. Bazeley was a keen fisherman who wrote several books about his favourite sport and though they are all out of print and largely forgotten now they include an account of a most strange day's grayling fishing high up in the Yorkshire Dales. Bazeley left Leeds early one morning in December and by the time he arrived at his favourite stream it was just getting light. Snow still lay on the ground and he relished the crisp, clean air after the fog of Leeds.

Having eaten a hearty breakfast in the local hotel, he walked the few miles to his favourite spot and began fishing. Within an hour he had nearly a dozen good grayling in his basket. And so it continued throughout the day. It seemed as if he could do no wrong.

With just a few days to go before Christmas he was lucky to get a room back at the hotel, but the fishing had been so prolific he could not bear to return to Leeds, which had originally been his plan.

Next morning he set off for the river again and fished down the first pool.

Immediately he was overtaken by a curious feeling, a feeling that someone else had just fished the same spot, yet he knew this was highly unlikely as he'd reached the riverbank just as the sun came up. A few moments later Bazeley landed a nice fish and decided to move further down the river. As he turned the next bend, where the stream rattled over golden pebbles, he saw a dark figure a few hundred yards ahead of him, kitted out in waders, rod over his shoulder and just leaving the pool to move downstream. Bazeley followed and fished the stream the old man had left. He did extremely well and caught several excellent grayling, but this was odd since the previous angler must have disturbed the water and in the general run of things he'd have been lucky to catch anything arriving so soon after someone else had left.

As Bazeley moved down to the next pitch, his bag already groaning under the weight of several fat grayling, he once again saw the old chap in front make a move. It was as if the old man, knowing the instant Bazeley made the decision to move, would each time make way for him.

This continued throughout the day but, judging by the superb sport Bazeley enjoyed, the old man's presence was, if anything, having a beneficial effect on the water. However, it was decidedly odd because, try as he might to vary the amount of time he spent on each pool, Bazeley always seemed to be the same distance behind the old man when he moved.

Dusk came on and Bazeley decided enough was enough. He packed up and walked slowly along the twisting, overgrown lane towards the hotel. To his delight he saw the old man from the river walking in the same direction. Perhaps, concluded Bazeley, he is staying in the same hotel and we will be able to talk fishing this evening. Bazeley hurried to catch up with the distant figure but failed. Then he saw the old man turn in at the door of the hotel and thought, 'Aha, I have him now!'

Moments later Bazeley was taking his boots off in the rod room.

'Where's the old man who's just come in?' he asked the landlord.

'Which one, sir?' came the reply.

'The old gentleman who just came in wearing thigh boots and carrying his tackle bags,' said Bazeley.

Bazeley was astonished at what came next.

'You must be mistaken, sir. You are the first fisherman we've had staying for more than three months.'

'But I saw him come in the door just a few minutes before me!' came Bazeley's astonished reply. He then gave a lengthy and detailed description of the fisherman whose steps he had dogged throughout the day.

The riverkeeper who had been standing nearby throughout the conversation spoke. 'Can you spare a moment?' he asked, indicating that Bazeley and he should retire to a quiet corner of the dark sitting room.

When they'd settled down on an old sofa by the fire the keeper spoke.

'The old chap you saw. I think you did see him right enough. He used to come and fish here for grayling every winter and he was just about the only one mad enough to fish every day whatever the conditions. We could never stop him even in the worst snow and frost. He had many narrow escapes over the years, but they never slowed him down. Then one day he failed to come back. He'd slipped into that pool by the willows. It was weather very much as it is now and Christmas was just as nearly upon us. Deep snow made the going difficult and no other angler would have been crazy enough to go out, so there was no one around to try to save him. We found him a few days later tangled up in the roots of an old willow and now every Christmas Eve he is seen fishing his favourite pools again.'

SPOONFED

ENGLAND, 1917

Two friends, one of whom was the writer J.H.R. Bazeley, were spinning for pike on a private lake in Yorkshire. They had landed half a dozen good pike by mid-afternoon when Bazeley's friend hooked a fish far bigger than anything they had encountered before. But after a battle lasting more than 20 minutes the line gave way and the fish was gone. When he reeled in, Bazeley's friend discovered that a knot had come undone and, cursing his stupidity for not tying it more carefully, he realised with some sadness that he had left a large silver spoon in the mouth of that pike. But the damage had been done and it was too late to correct it. Bazeley's friend merely resolved to check and double check his tackle in future. The two men did their best to hide it, but they were crestfallen as the lost fish was quite clearly one of the really big – and rarely caught – specimens for which the lake was at that time famous. There was nothing for it except to keep fishing, which they did until darkness fell and they returned to their hotel with their catch, but determined to try again the next day.

Just after dawn the following morning they pushed their boat out through the reeds and quietly let the anchor down through the green water. They cast out their baits, smoked their pipes and awaited events. An hour later, with hardly a ripple to disturb the surface of the lake, the two men decided to haul anchor and try elsewhere. Bazeley lifted his rod and began to reel in. Immediately he felt the weight of a very good fish. He played it carefully, not wishing for a repeat of yesterday's disaster, and soon a great, gleaming pike that looked almost 1 yard (91.4cm) long rolled at the surface and admitted defeat. The moment it was in the net Bazeley looked down and saw that his hook, which had originally been attached to a sprat, had gone through the eye of a large silver spoon that was firmly lodged in the pike's jaws. The silver spoon was unquestionably the one his friend had been using the day before. This was the very same pike they had lost the previous day.

Bazeley seems to have been peculiarly blessed with this kind of incredible luck. A few years earlier he had been broken by a big pike early in the day only to catch the same pike that afternoon. On this occasion he had not been fishing for pike at all. He'd been using gut not wire, and the pike had easily bitten through it. But in the afternoon, still using gut, his hook had caught in the eye of the hook he'd lost in the fish's mouth that morning. With one metal hook making a link with the other, the pike had been unable to reach the gut line with its teeth and was easily landed.

SEEING IS BELIEVING

ENGLAND, 1919

The writer Arthur Ransome used regularly to fish the River Lune in Lancashire. It was one of his favourite rivers, particularly at that time in the autumn when the green of summer was just turning to gold. He also liked the river then because low, clear water meant he was far more aware of what life was like for the fish in the river.

An autumn day on the Lune was to produce one of Ransome's most remarkable fishing experiences.

He arrived at the river and noted that he could see the leaves rolling along the bottom. He set up a light trout rod and the lightest cast in his wallet – given the conditions, nothing else would be likely to produce a fish. He cast out and was able to watch his minnow spin across the pool. It sparkled as it crossed the dark background of the riverbed. At times he checked his retrieve so that the little spinner did not tangle with the leaves that tumbled now and then through the water.

He tried the first pool he came to and then moved down to a position just below a footbridge. Here a deeper pool flowed more steadily between two slack areas either side of the stream. As he was about to cast out his minnow, Ransome thought he saw a flash deep in the darkest part of the fast-flowing river. He cast out into the slack water, reeled in until the minnow was whirled away by the fast water and then watched as his lure swung across through the deeper stream. A big fish rose and followed the minnow but did not take.

The minnow came in safely but Ransome continued to watch the spot where he'd seen the fish. Something extraordinary was starting. The minnow seemed to have altered the whole mood of the pool. He saw a second fish move and then a third and a fourth. They flashed and twirled again and again. Ransome sent his spinner among them once more and their twisting and cavorting became faster and more urgent.

With the next cast the water seemed to become filled with big salmon dancing together. Still the minnow was not taken. Ransome tried again but he was so astonished at the dancing salmon that he forgot to watch his minnow and only realised something was amiss when he felt his line rapidly running out. He lifted his rod and knew that he had hooked a salmon. Now a salmon on a little trout rod can be landed, but it is not easy. Ransome's fish immediately tried to get down to the next pool and with his toothpick rod Ransome knew he could not stop it. The only thing to do was to run down the river with the fish, and this is what he did.

When Ransome caught up with his fish it had reached a much shallower stretch of the river. He could see it plainly and realised – almost with relief, given his inadequate tackle – that it was at least manageable. About 10lb (4.5kg), he thought.

The salmon came over towards Ransome and into a smooth, shallow stretch of water where it was clearly visible. He then noticed a much larger salmon swimming alongside his fish. With a renewed burst of energy Ransome's salmon suddenly made a dash for a series of rapids below the pool. Half running and half falling, Ransome just managed to keep up, but even as his fish tore down through the rough water Ransome was aware that the bigger fish was right next to it.

In the calmer waters below, Ransome watched his salmon rub its nose on a rock. Immediately beside it the bigger salmon had taken up its station. Ransome's salmon then moved down the water until it was just below him. The other salmon was circling around the line. Moments later it turned in the current and allowed itself to be carried down broadside on against the cast above Ransome's salmon's head. Ransome suddenly felt the massive extra pull on his rod and had to yield line quickly to avoid a break. Both fish were swept away down the river and Ransome followed once again. In the end Ransome did land his fish, but it was only in the last few seconds of the fight that the bigger salmon finally moved away.

For years afterwards Ransome wondered if the big fish had consciously been trying to save its smaller cousin. There was no way to be sure but relying on the evidence of his own eyes Ransome came to believe that really was what had happened.

LOST RING

ENGLAND, 1920

Fishermen are notorious for losing things. Every year thousands of baitdroppers, fly boxes, rods and reels are left on riverbanks and lakesides. Fishermen who wade regularly are prone to drop watches, rings, hats and flies into the water and it is very rare indeed for them ever to be found. But it does happen and every now and then it happens in the most extraordinary fashion.

A fisherman who came every year from London to try for the salmon in the North Tyne was in the habit of taking his gold signet ring off each morning and putting it safely in a drawer before setting out for the river. Then came the fateful morning when he forgot and on reaching the river and beginning to wade, he discovered that he was still wearing the ring. He was a superstitious man and as he'd always caught plenty of fish while not wearing the ring he was not going to risk everything by keeping it on today.

He tucked his rod under his arm, carefully slipped the ring off his finger, felt for his shirt pocket and dropped the ring – straight into the river. He saw it glint for an instant and then it was gone. The ring was not particularly valuable but it had enormous sentimental value and the fisherman was not prepared to lose it without a fight. All thoughts of fishing vanished as he took his rod and began his search. The water where he was wading was not particularly deep, but it was fast-flowing and the golden gravel on the bottom made the perfect camouflage for a gold ring.

The fisherman tried dropping stones that he thought were of similar weight to the ring in order to see how far downstream they travelled before reaching the bottom. He then raked over the area with his wading stick. Nothing. The search continued and he increased his distance gradually from the spot where the ring was lost in case the current had carried it further than he'd first thought. Still nothing. Hours later and too despondent to fish at all, the fisherman returned to the cottage he'd rented.

He searched again the next day, having carefully marked the spot where he'd first waded, but still no sign of the ring could be found. The fisherman tried to forget his loss and continue with his fishing holiday but somehow it was spoilt and he left early to return to London.

His landlord happened to call in on the day the fisherman was packing up to leave and he nodded sympathetically when he heard the story, but expressed the hope that the fisherman, despite this disaster, would return for his annual holiday the following year.

One year later the fisherman drove up to the door of the cottage he'd rented now for ten consecutive years. He'd almost forgotten the lost ring and was looking forward to a week on a river that, from reports he'd received earlier, he knew was in excellent order. He parked his car, opened the front door of the cottage and turned on the light. Just as he threw his bags down he saw it. The ring he'd lost the year before was right in the middle of the hall table. The fisherman simply couldn't believe it. He rang the estate lodge and spoke to the manager who explained that another visitor fishing the same stretch of river just a few weeks ago had hooked it. He'd thought this such a remarkable occurrence that he'd mentioned it to the estate manager who immediately remembered the tale of the missing ring.

Perhaps the most curious aspect of the story is that the fisherman who caught the ring had been fishing almost half a mile (800m) downstream from the point at which the ring had originally been lost.

TWINS

ENGLAND, 1925

It's a mathematical truism that given the number of people in the world and the number of recorded events worldwide it would be a remarkable coincidence if most of us at some time in our lives did not experience an extraordinary coincidence. That meticulous recorder of 30 years' fishing on the Herefordshire Wye, J. Arthur Hutton, noted a fair few chance happenings that seem – on the face of it – quite unbelievable, but none more so than one autumn morning in 1925 when he fished the Carrot's Pool.

He'd fished for some time without success and was about to move to the next pool, when a good fish head-and-tailed at the head of the Carrot's. He covered it and next minute was struggling with a large fresh fish that cartwheeled and leapt for all it was worth before it came to the net. The very next cast he was into another fish that fought exactly as the first fish had fought. Twenty minutes later the second fish was in the net. When they were laid out side by side Hutton was astonished to discover that the two salmon were to all intents and purposes identical. He took them back to the fishing hut and found that each fish weighed precisely 25lb 7½oz (11.6kg).

UP BEFORE THE BEAK

ENGLAND, 1926

An elderly Devon landowner, who also happened to be the leading local aristocrat, lord lieutenant of the county and master of the local pack of harriers, was one of those landowners still convinced, like his eighteenth-century ancestors, that a gentleman should be allowed to do exactly what he likes on his own property. He owned a big lake that was fed by a tributary from the River Teign and the tributary was the most important part of the whole river system for spawning trout. But the old landowner took no account of this. If other landowners and fishermen relied on the trout in the old man's tributary being left in peace so that their bits of river would have a good head of trout then that was their problem; it was of no concern to the leading local aristocrat. But on a more positive note the old boy could be rather paternalistic if it suited him.

One feature of this paternalistic streak had become something of an annual event. Every year for as long as he could remember the old man had invited every child in the local village to come and enjoy the most wonderful day's fishing, a day that infuriated all his neighbours and every adult fisherman for 20 miles (32.2km) in every direction.

The problem was that the old man did not invite the children to fish his lake or even his tributary. Instead, when the trout from the Teign came up the tributary in their droves to spawn the old man opened the sluice gates on his pond and flooded his meadows. This was great for the meadows because it produced an early and rich crop of grass, but it was disastrous for the trout. As the waters receded the trout found themselves stranded in the meadow and it was at this moment that the old man invited all the local children to fish. Hundreds of children splashed about the meadow wrestling and kicking the fish into submission, and any trout they could catch by any means they were entitled to keep.

As all this went on the old man no doubt wandered about looking very pleased with himself, but the day of reckoning was not far off. The old man was reported to the board of conservators – a group of respectable citizens charged with looking after the river. They were outraged at the old man's behaviour and told him that the meadow fishing must stop. The old man was equally outraged at this affront to the liberty of the trueborn Englishman and told the board of conservators they could go to hell.

'The ponds are mine. The land is mine. The tributary is mine and by God the trout are mine!' he is reported to have shouted at anyone who would listen. But it did no good. He held his meadow fishing day again and was duly summoned to appear before the local magistrate. Red-faced and apoplectic with rage he stood in the dock and predicted (accurately as it happens) the downfall of Empire. He was fined one shilling and the frenzied meadow splash was held no more.

WARM-WATER SURPRISE

ENGLAND, 1926

Most people think of the cod – if they think of it at all – as an average-sized fish that mostly ends up fried and wrapped in newspaper. In fact in earlier times cod were prized not just for their abundance, but also for the fact that, occasionally, individual specimens might weigh up to 100lb (45.4kg) or more. These giant mother cod, as they were known, were wiped out by huge factory ships and over-fishing in the 1960s, but at least one angler managed to hook one before the glory days of cod fishing came to an end and he did it in the most spectacular fashion.

Our cod angler was out fishing off the northeast coast of England in the mid-1920s. He was a veteran of the Great War and had lost an eye and part of one hand at Ypres, but he never allowed his wounds to get in the way of his fishing. He'd been a fanatical angler before the war and when the hostilities were over he went back to his boat and his rods and lines.

He always fished the same marks. One or two were just a few hundred yards offshore; others up to 1 mile (1.6km) away. On this bright sunny spring day he decided on a mark he hadn't tried for some time. He was hoping to catch a good bag of cod because he liked to distribute his fish, if he'd had a good day, to elderly friends in his home village.

Now our northern fisherman was very experienced. When he hooked a cod he usually knew straight away that it was a cod. There was something about the cod's first strong plunge followed by its complete capitulation that was absolutely unique to the species. As well as cod he occasionally caught coalfish, whiting and even, on one occasion, a salmon, but mostly it was cod with which, he told his friends, he'd conducted a lifelong love affair.

The boat moved slowly across the mark with the running tide. His heavy weight whipped the line from his reel and perhaps 20 seconds later he felt the lead begin to bump along the bottom. Then 'Thump!' Something had hit the mackerel-tail bait with a vengeance. It was a very good cod for the area – at a little over 15lb (6.8kg) it was one of the best he'd ever caught. This was a great start to the day and he was delighted.

Back over the side went his strip of mackerel and soon, once again, he felt the satisfying bump of lead against the sandy bed of the sea. Then something odd happened. He felt the lead stop as if his hook had fouled something completely immovable. Then there was a great rush as something heavy and powerful moved rapidly against the tide. Ten minutes later the biggest cod the fisherman had ever seen in his life came flapping over the gunwales. It weighed over 60lb (27.2kg) – how much over the fisherman never discovered as his scales stopped at 60lb and having no interest in records he knocked the fish on the head and gutted it there and then.

He carried on fishing and soon more than a dozen big cod lay in the bottom of the boat. It was mid-afternoon now and plenty of time remained so he continued to fish. At three o'clock another big fish hit the bait and for an instant the fisherman thought he'd hooked another giant mother cod, but there was something very different about this one. This was a powerful, dogged swimmer with none of the sudden capitulation that characterised the cod's battle tactics.

Twenty minutes into the arm-aching struggle the fisherman realised that this was almost certainly a species he had never before encountered. He was sure it wasn't a giant conger eel; it couldn't possibly be a shark. Precisely one hour later the fish reached the surface. To the fisherman's eternal astonishment he discovered he'd hooked and landed a tuna fish!

In fact, when the fish first came aboard the fisherman had no idea what it was. It was only two hours after arriving back at his home village that someone was found who could identify the 80lb (36.3kg) fish.

Quite a number of tuna were caught off the British Isles in the 1920s, but they are now endangered and highly protected. It seems that small increases in the average temperature of the Gulf Stream waters during that decade encouraged stray tuna to wander much further north than they ever would normally. But to catch a giant cod – a cold water species – on the same day as a tuna must be unique in the annals of fishing history.

SWIMMING TO VICTORY
ENGLAND, 1927

Carp fishermen are notorious for their eccentricity. Why this should be no one seems to know, but numerous writers have tried to explain. Perhaps it has something to do with the dark, secret, hidden lakes where carp tend to be found; perhaps it has something to do with the long hours one has to spend at the lakeside if one is to have any chance of catching a good carp. Among some carp fishermen it is a matter of pride that they should, for example, have spent a whole week fishing all day and all night with absolutely no result. Of course, they would argue that this is the only way to have even the remotest chance of catching a really big carp. And carp do reach staggering sizes. The British record stands a little over 50lb (22.7kg) and a fish of that size would cover a dining-room table. On the Continent carp grow to twice that size and in carp fishing circles there is always a feeling that such a carp might well exist in some forgotten lake deep in the English countryside.

So the carp is a creature of mystery and enormous power. When it captivates the fisher he or she is usually captivated for life and this passion for carp fishing has produced some splendid days.

A little-known lake in Herefordshire contains some of Britain's biggest and wiliest carp and it was here that an enormous fish was landed way back in the 1920s – but only after a bizarre struggle of titanic proportions.

The fisherman was the local postman. He'd fished the lake for many years and caught many carp up to about 12lb (5.4kg), but the giants of the lake had always eluded him. He'd seen them often enough on balmy nights in June when they drifted in among the trailing willows or cruised the edges of the reed beds, but long and hard as he fished he could never make contact. One or two of his friends had come trembling to him when they met together in the evenings in the local pub and told tales of being smashed in an instant by something vast, fast and powerful. The local vicar had been closest of all to landing one of these leviathans. He'd hooked his giant at dusk on the opening night of the season and by some miracle his tackle survived the first unstoppable rush of the huge fish. Later on, the vicar described how the surface of the lake seemed to rise as the great carp surged up and away. Its first run took nearly 200 yards (183m) of 15-pound breaking strain line from the vicar's reel and it was only a happy accident that prevented an instant break. The vicar, desperately trying to stay in control of the fish and leaping about the muddy bank in the process, slipped and fell. In that instant he dropped his rod and the fish, thinking one assumes that it had got clear, stopped in its tracks. When the vicar got back on his feet and picked up his rod he assumed that the fish would be long gone, but by a miracle it was still there and the battle continued. Again and again the fish rushed towards a distant sunken tree and on the third rush there was nothing the vicar could do. The carp crashed into the sunken roots and branches and the line parted.

When the postman heard this tale his obsession with carp fishing grew deeper and stronger. He spent more and more time by the side of the lake. He stayed up all night to fish and did his rounds in a trance-like state of sleeplessness. Then when he least expected something to happen he hooked what he later described as a carp the size of a pig.

He had been setting off for home, but as he wandered along the lakeside before turning up the lane to the village he saw a vast, dark shadow moving slowly across the gravel in just 3ft (0.9m) of clear water. He froze and then retraced his steps. Luckily he had not yet dismantled his rod. He found the biggest worm in his tin, tied it to his hook and crept slowly back to the exact spot from which he'd seen the fish.

Carp can be spooked by the least movement, so the postman inched his way forward and it seemed an age before he was back within sight of the water's edge. The postman had been certain that the fish would have departed, but it was still there, lying doggo on the bottom with an occasional twitch of a fin the only evidence that it was alive.

The postman was shaking as he gently swung his worm out over the water. It dropped with an echoing splash just behind the fish. Instantly the great carp turned and the

worm vanished into the fish's giant mouth. The postman was so astonished that at first he did absolutely nothing. Then instinct took over and he lifted his rod sharply into the air.

What happened next was like being attached to an express train. The vicar's experiences flashed momentarily through the postman's mind as the great fish soared away across the lake, water bow-waving from its back.

Luckily he'd hooked the fish in the most open part of the lake. To reach an area of dense rushes it would have to turn back towards the postman, which it was very unlikely to do. The only other area of sanctuary was 300–400 yards (274–366m) away on the far side of the lake. The fish opted to put as much distance between it and the fisherman as possible. The first run was devastating and when the postman looked down at his reel he saw that he was rapidly running out of line. Then he did something that he himself could not later explain. He walked into the lake and began to swim after the carp. He was fully clothed, but simply could not bear to lose this fish after waiting so many years for just such a specimen.

As he moved slowly out across the lake he remembered how the vicar had told him he stopped his giant carp's first rush. The postman lowered his rod until his line went slack, hoping that the fish would think it had got off and slow down. The trick worked and it gave the postman the chance to regain some line.

By this time the fish was a long way off, but the postman knew he couldn't rush things. Treading water and keeping in touch only lightly with the fish, he drifted towards the opposite bank and his seemingly docile quarry. All the time as he moved forward he regained line. At least if the fish made another rush he would be ready. And then it happened. At first he was aware that however much line he reeled in he could not regain contact with the great surging fish. He reeled faster and faster and then realised that the fish was coming back towards him. A second later the fish shot past just a few feet away, heading directly for the bank the postman had just left. This was worrying because much of that bank was lined with thick beds of rushes. If the fish reached them it would be lost. The postman turned and began to swim after the fish once again.

The second run was, if anything, even more powerful than the first and the postman knew that this fish was old enough and big enough to know that sanctuary lay anywhere where reeds or roots or sunken branches would help it throw the hook. The postman tried everything. He tried to make the fish think it had got free by dropping his rod; he tried to put side strain on it to turn it away from the distant reeds, but all to no avail. The carp reached the rushes and bored deep into them.

Most fishermen would have given up at this point, but not the postman. He swam to the reed bed, grabbed the line at the point where it disappeared from view into the water and ran his hand down it until he felt what he thought was the fish's head. He then got both hands down and around the body of the fish, which was firmly wedged in the reeds and could no longer bolt, and lifted it bodily into his arms.

Covered completely in mud and slime the postman half swam and half staggered to the bank, where he collapsed with the fish under him. The biggest carp ever caught from the lake was his. The story went from village to village and though one or two die-hards thought the swimming postman's technique was a little unsporting he was hailed as a hero by most. The carp weighed 28lb (12.7kg) and was by far the largest anyone locally had ever seen or heard of.

DEFINITELY
NOT A SALMON

SCOTLAND, 1928

A fisherman on the Thurso had spent a long, hot June day catching poorly recovered and still rather black salmon kelts. But he had also landed one good fresh 14-pounder (6.4kg) and was reluctant to stop fishing before the light failed. He'd long given up using the fly, but had kept his Jock Scott tied on to his cast and simply added a couple of big lobworms. Once more he cast his worms into the foamy water at the head of the pool and felt them bounce around along the gravelly bottom. Then, just as the bait reached the shallow water at the tail of the pool, the fisherman felt a long, slow pull. He struck hard and was once again into a heavy fish.

'Damn,' he mumbled. 'Another big old kelt.'

The fish was so slow-moving it was like being attached to a huge log but, eager to get the pointless battle over as soon as possible, the fisherman put as much pressure on the fish as he dared. Ten minutes passed and still the huge fish hugged the bottom and moved slowly up and down the pool.

The fisherman shouted to his gillie that he thought he'd hooked a 40lb (18.1kg) kelt. Still the battle continued. Then the fish stopped moving around and stayed absolutely still for 20 minutes. The poor fisherman's arm felt as though it was about to be pulled out of its socket. Convinced it was just a huge old kelt, the gillie threw a rock into the water and the fish began its slow patrol once again. The minutes passed, then after almost an hour, the fish left the bottom and began to come towards the surface. From the depths came a horrifying sight – what seemed like yards of undulating fish thrashed the surface of the pool for a moment before disappearing once again from view. The huge salmon was an eel – and a truly enormous eel at that.

The fisherman's main fear, now that he knew what he was attached to, was that his friend the river manager would come along and see him fighting with this monstrous thing. He sent the gillie to keep an eye out lest his friend should observe him looking a complete fool with an eel apparently caught on a Jock Scott.

The gillie waved the all-clear and the drama recommenced with the eel having descended to the depths once again. 'The strength of that eel was quite unbelievable,' said the fisherman later on, but for now there was nothing he could do short of pulling for a break. But he was reluctant to lose that Jock Scott – it was a favourite that had produced some superb fish.

Finally the great eel began to tire, but the gillie could neither net nor gaff it. After several failed attempts the fisherman, despairing of victory, put his rod down and began hauling the line in hand over hand. Slowly the eel was pulled towards a flat rock where the gillie waited. As the eel's head was drawn over the rock the gillie opened a huge pocket knife and cut it off. The eel's head came bouncing to the shore, but its body slipped back into the water, still writhing horribly. Within seconds the whole of the pool was dyed bright pink. The rocks were covered in blood and slime and the Jock Scott, long the pride of its owner, was beyond all hope of recovery.

To add insult to injury, the fisherman and gillie had to spend almost half an hour scrubbing the blood and slime from the rocks. Having done that, they recovered the body of the eel and estimated its live weight at an incredible 10lb (4.5kg) – a huge size for an eel. The fisherman was exhausted and decided enough was enough.

But that huge eel is probably the biggest ever apparently caught on a salmon fly.

DON'T SPARE THE ROD

SCOTLAND, 1928

It is often said that the reason worm fishing is frequently banned for salmon and trout is that these fish are so stupid they are too easily caught on this bait. To give the fish a chance we have to use more difficult techniques – by which is usually meant a scrap of fur, feather and tinsel tied to a baitless hook.

The stupidity of salmon when in a serious taking mood can be judged by the experience of G.P.R. Balfour-Kinnear one morning in the late 1920s.

He was casting into a strong headwind on a big river and the effort of throwing rod and line forward each time meant that now and then the tip of his rod hit the water after the line sailed away ahead of it. Mr Balfour-Kinnear knew the salmon would be taking that day – conditions were perfect apart from the strong wind, and he was determined not to give up until he had a fish on the bank.

After a few hours he was still fishing in earnest but without the least hint that a fish had shown any interest in his fly. He decided to have one more cast before moving to another pool. The rod did its work, the line sailed out over the water and the tip of the rod once again dipped into the water at the end of the cast. Immediately, an enormous salmon broke the surface like a sounding whale, took the top of the rod in its mouth and tried to pull it down into the deep. The fish hung on for a few seconds before realising its mistake.

Balfour-Kinnear stood speechless and immobile for the next 20 minutes and, despite the fact that he did not get a fish that day, he dined out on the story of the rod-eating salmon for many years after.

SLIPPERY CUSTOMER

SCOTLAND, 1929

There are many tales of salmon jumping into rowing boats. The occurrence is not so unusual because when conditions are perfect, hundreds, perhaps thousands, of salmon will move quickly upriver together and, as they jump obstacles along the way, individuals may make an occasional misjudgement and end up not on the other side of an obstacle, but on a dinner plate.

Occasionally a salmon being played by an angler will rush at the boat, leap and end up in the very place it was trying very hard to escape, but what might look like a suicide bid on the part of a fish can sometimes help it break free.

The *Dundee Advertiser* ran a story about just such an occurrence. A fisherman had been playing a good salmon for more than 40 minutes and he was convinced the worst was over and the fish would soon be his, so he was only slightly perturbed when he felt the line go slack and realised that the fish was making a run towards rather than away from the boat.

He reeled in frantically to try to make contact again but it was too late, and before he realised what was happening, the fish had leapt from the water and landed in the boat. The result was chaos as the gillie dropped his oars to try to secure the fish while the fisherman dropped his rod to try to help. The fisherman had one end of the salmon, the gillie the other, but the boat was rocking from side to side, the two men were shouting encouragement to each other and they perhaps forgot that they were dealing with a fish that still had plenty of strength left; suddenly, with a flick of its tail the fish bounced out of their hands, hit the side of the boat and toppled into the water, in the process breaking the cast.

For a full ten minutes, the curses of both men could be heard a mile away.

DIRTY MONEY
ENGLAND, 1930

Right through the 1920s and 1930s the owner of a fishing hotel in Devon gained a reputation for eccentricity. She had continued to run the hotel after the death of her husband but as the years passed she became increasingly irascible and began to treat even the grandest of her customers with ill-concealed contempt.

However, she had her favourites and if she liked someone she would reduce their bill. Those she treated coldly would often find strange items had been added to their invoice, but if the total was queried the landlady would make sarcastic remarks or suggest that her customer might like to try a different hotel next time he fancied a fishing holiday in Devon.

Here her customers found themselves in a difficult position for this hotel had the very best fishing for miles around, which is why they came back again and again and put up with haughty glances, withering looks and inflated bills.

As the years went by the landlady's eccentricities grew more pronounced and there were days when her guests would do anything to avoid meeting her in a corridor or on the stairs. In the mornings they left early for the river, but even at 5a.m. she might be standing at the front door mumbling about muddy boots or incompetent casting or even that a particular angler would have to stop coming because he was too tall, too short or had a moustache that made him look untrustworthy.

Occasionally her rudeness was so cunning and bizarre that her regular guests chuckled at her audacity, while her favourites sighed with relief that they were among the chosen. To an outsider it must have seemed extraordinary that a little old woman could so terrorise a mixed bag of 20 or more middle-aged London barristers, land agents and retired colonels.

Her greatest triumph came one spring morning when a grand guest who'd stayed for three days and enjoyed some very successful days on the river was about to leave. Like most visitors he'd come down by rail and hoped to catch the 7.45 evening train back to London. This was precisely the time that many of the other guests would be certain to be found milling around near the hotel reception prior to dinner. The grand guest presented himself at reception, and having waited ten minutes for the landlady to notice him, asked for his bill. When she gave it to him he made the fundamental mistake of checking. Regulars – of which he was not one – knew that this was a fatal error and there was a shocked, audible intake of breath from those waiting to go in to dinner at the moment he began to pore over the little piece of paper.

Now this was in the days when hotels charged separately for baths and the grand guest found that he had been billed for three baths – one for each day of his stay. But he had been so keen on his fishing and so exhausted every evening that in fact he had not had a single bath. He objected to these additions to his bill. The room fell completely silent. One or two guests ducked and ran. The landlady fixed the grand guest with a stony stare. He, oblivious to her reputation, said again that he'd been overcharged. It was at this second offence that the landlady spoke up in a loud voice.

'So you've been in my hotel among all my fishing gentlemen for three days and you haven't had a bath.' The grand guest grew pale and began to tremble. The landlady scented blood. She shouted down the back stairs to one of the servants. 'Did you hear that, Doris? This gentleman has been here three days and he hasn't had a single bath. What do you think of that? I think it's disgusting.' The grand guest, who was used to ordering servants about, plunged his hand into his pocket, pulled out a wad of notes and threw them down. He then ran for it and, despite the quality of the fishing, that was one hotel he never patronised again.

SEA TROUT
TO SET YOUR WATCH BY

SCOTLAND, 1930

Scotland's River Shiel is a river of which it is said a man either loves or loathes it. George Brennand, who fished it from the 1930s on for many years, always said that to fish it one must enjoy the sounds of ghosts and ghouls, the sound of lonely bagpipes played at some unearthly hour in some forgotten cottage. But for the man unperturbed by strange nocturnal sights and sounds the Shiel was a sporting river with few equals. It is and always was a night-fishing river; a place for big sea trout and plenty of them.

George Brennand recalled that the fish showed no interest before 10.30 in summer and more usually it was 11.30 before the fisherman could expect any action. But when the sport was good it was very good indeed. Brennand arrived at a spot called the Cliffe on the first night of a week's holiday and at precisely 10.45 – and by precisely he meant just as the second hand ticked past the 12 – he hooked and landed a sea trout of 4lb (1.8kg). The next night – again as the second hand swept past the 12 – he hooked and landed a sea trout of 5lb (2.3kg). The following night at 10.45p.m. he did it again, this time with a fish of 4lb (1.8kg).

Each sea trout took the same fly – a big Invicta – in precisely the same spot.

CASTING AT THE SAVOY

ENGLAND, 1930

Two Americans staying in London had an argument over whether or not it would be possible to cast a fly from the roof of their hotel – the Savoy – over the gardens and the busy Embankment and into the Thames.

They were so determined to settle the dispute that they went along to Hardy Brothers, the tackle-makers, and asked them to decide if such a thing was possible. Hardy Brothers approached the angler and author Esmond Drury, who agreed to attempt the feat on condition that he was tied securely to a chimney on the hotel roof.

Early one Sunday morning, with the help of a policeman who stopped all the traffic on the Embankment, he proved that it was indeed possible to cast a fly into the Thames from the roof of the Savoy.

TWO TIMES UNLUCKY

IRELAND, 1932

It's very rare for a fisherman to hook a really huge salmon – say, over 60lb (27.2kg) – but to have hooked two such fish must be unique. It happened to a friend of the writer G.D. Luard.

Luard and his friend were fishing the Cummeragh at a place that was normally a pretty poor bet for a salmon, but every now and then it turned up trumps. Luard himself had three salmon in a day from the stream and then his friend hooked the giant.

Now both Luard and his friend had caught plenty of salmon over 30lb (13.6kg); they had caught a few over 40lb (18.1kg) so they knew a great deal about very big salmon. When Luard's friend Dick cast his Prawn over what seemed a pretty unexceptional rise he could not have known that he was in for the biggest battle – and the biggest disappointment – of his life.

No sooner had the Prawn hit the water than the line began to run out. The pull was smooth but almost quivering. Being an experienced salmon fisher Dick waited before striking to try to ensure that he achieved the best possible hook hold. After what seemed like an age Dick lifted his rod and the fight began. The fish at first ran upstream and then stayed absolutely still in the fast water at the neck of the pool. The ease with which it held station told the two men that this was no ordinary fish. The line hummed as it vibrated in the fierce current. Then the fish slipped into the stream and, turning, came back down rapidly and past the shingle spit on which the anglers were standing. In what seemed a completely effortless manner it then took out 80 yards (73.2m) of line before taking up station once again, only now at the very end of the stream. Just below was a stretch of rough fast water. Fearing that the fish might reach this part of the stream Dick applied more pressure. It had the opposite effect and the great salmon began to edge towards the racing, tumbling falls.

If the fish reached this water all would be over as it led into a long, fierce stretch known as the Whirls and every fish that had made it to this bit of water in the past had been lost. What were they to do?

Luard ran down the bank to get below the fish. He then waded out and threw stones to discourage it from going further downstream, but the tactic had no effect and slowly but surely the huge salmon – for by now they were certain it was huge – slipped towards the tumbling water. As it approached the shallow rapids the salmon stopped again and held station. The fish was just 25ft (7.6m) from the two fishermen and clearly visible in the shallow, clear water. Nothing would move it and Luard thought of trying to sneak up on him and gaff him. But the fish would almost certainly see him, panic and be gone. Five minutes passed. Then up out of the shallow water came the biggest tail either man had ever seen and the tail was more than 4ft (1.2m) behind the point where the line entered the water at the fish's head. The tail flicked lazily, the fish turned and vanished, rocketing down through the rapids towards the Whirls. With a loud twang the line snapped. The two men were too upset even to speak.

Luard estimated that fish at well over 60lb (27.1kg) and if anything he was inclined, as a rule, to underestimate the weight of his fish.

Some time after the loss of this great fish Luard was

once again fishing the same stream with his friend Dick. They were at a place where a pool opened out just below an old bridge. Immediately below the bridge the water was shallow but it deepened quickly until it reached a smooth, heavy bend where it was very deep indeed. Here in the dark depths huge salmon were known to take up residence but they were hardly ever in the taking mood. The deep pool was normally fished from a boat, but Luard and his friend had arrived on foot so Dick waded out to a position from which it was just possible to fish the pool. While this went on the gillie set off upstream to bring the boat. Luard settled down with his pipe on the grassy bank, while out in front and in fairly deep water his friend began spinning. After just a few casts Dick shouted that he had hooked a fish. Luard jumped to his feet and glimpsed what he later described as the biggest fish he had ever seen in his life. It came up like a great long log, stayed on the surface for a few seconds and then sank from view.

Dick was using a powerful rod and his strongest tackle, but slowly and steadily, despite maximum pressure, the fish made its way down the river in a manner identical to the great fish he'd lost earlier. Luard estimated this fish at almost twice the length of a 30-pounder (13.6kg). Dick said afterwards that he had never felt anything like the force of this fish. Luard only commented that throughout the fight he had a sixth sense that this fish was just too big to be landed on rod and line. There was something inevitable about its eventual loss.

The fish had gone 50 yards (45.7m), 80 (73.2m), 90 (82.3m). Nothing could stop him. Dick followed until the water reached to within 1in (2.5cm) of the top of his chest waders. Any increase in pressure simply made the fish increase its pace. Dick, unable to go any further for fear of flooding his waders, shouted for the boat. They heard the gillie's distant reply, but it was unlikely that he would reach them in time. By now more than 200 yards (183m) of line had been taken from the reel and Dick looked down to see just a few turns of backing remaining on the spool. The rod bent further and further until its tip almost touched the water. Then, just at the point where it seemed the rod would burst under the pressure, the line gave way at the reel and the fish was gone. Normally that would have been the end of the tale, but the line was new and well greased. It would almost certainly float and there was a slim chance, if they were quick enough, that they could find it. Dick hopped into the boat with the gillie and they set off in pursuit of the fish. Against all the odds they spotted the end of the line and managed to thread it back through the rings and tie it securely to the reel. So much line had been lost that it took some time for Dick to reel in sufficiently to see if the fish was still there. It was. But as soon as it felt the pressure of the powerful salmon rod it began, as before, to make its steady but unstoppable way downstream. But now he was in the boat Dick at least had a chance.

A few hundred yards below the pool where the fish was hooked was a massive overhanging limestone cliff. If the fish reached this spot it would be almost impossible to control. Somehow the men in the boat knew that the deep, difficult water beneath the cliff was precisely the spot for which the fish was heading. Luard was so convinced that this salmon had the battle all mapped out in its head that he later said that if all salmon behaved in the same way salmon fishing would become unthinkable.

The fish reached the cliff pool. Dick leapt from the boat and tried to play the salmon from the shingle bank opposite the deep, dangerous stretch of water. For a while the fish appeared to be manageable. It stayed deep and was quite immovable, but Dick knew that all the time it stayed put it was tiring. Then with a burst of speed that Dick had never encountered before, the fish sped away and out towards the deepest water beneath the cliff. The line thrummed and sang in the wind as Dick applied as much pressure as he could, but the line cut ever closer to the cliff edge and the fish bored effortlessly deeper. Then, in an instant, it was over. The line fell slack on the water and when Dick reeled in he found that it had been clean cut through a few feet above the hook.

Estimating the size of fish is always difficult, but both Luard and his friend had caught very big fish in the past. They had seen this fish several times during the tussle and were convinced it was well over 4ft (1.2m) and probably closer to 5ft (1.5m) in length. It was also an unusually deep fish.

Luard hated the idea that fishermen had a reputation for exaggerating the size of the one that got away, so publicly he put the lost fish down at a minimum of 60lb (27.2kg). In private he was convinced, as was his friend, that the fish was far more likely to have weighed over 70lb (31.8kg). Had it been landed it would certainly have been a new British record salmon. It would also have been the biggest fish ever landed from fresh water on rod and line. The principal reason the two friends were so certain that this had been a truly massive fish was that, despite their experience with large salmon and the strength of their tackle, they were never really in contention. At no time during the battle had the fish shown signs of tiring; at no time was Dick able to deflect that salmon from its course even for an instant. And there was something truly uncanny about the fish's unhurried, purposeful plan of escape. A plan that, from the very beginning, was bound to succeed.

BEGINNER'S LUCK

SCOTLAND, 1935

The phrase 'beginner's luck' and fishing seem to go hand in hand. There are countless stories of complete novices landing superb fish, but that is part of the charm of fishing. There are also several recorded instances of people who had never fished in their lives being persuaded to try just one cast and then hooking and landing massive fish. Normally this would lead to a lifelong enthusiasm for fishing, but not always. One or two anglers have been known to catch a fish on their very first cast and then never fish again.

But perhaps the most amazing tale of beginner's luck happened to a youngster fishing one of Scotland's best-known rivers for the first time. The youngster had no experience of fly fishing and had tried spinning on only one previous occasion when a friend had lent him a rod. When he set out to spin the Spey he used borrowed tackle.

He was with a party of friends all of whom were highly experienced salmon fishers. The experts went to various pools and the youngster wandered farther afield and was left to his own devices. At the first place he stopped he saw a salmon rise just 20ft (6.1m) out in the stream. He cast his spinner out towards it, but the spinner fell well short of the target. Disappointed at his failure the young man began to reel in, but hardly had he begun to turn the handle of the reel than everything went solid. He thought he'd hooked the bottom until the bottom began to move.

He shouted at the top of his voice and, luckily, one of his friends was sufficiently close to hear his cries. Soon several of his friends had come running. Despite their apparent haste they were convinced he really had either hooked the bottom or was engaged in a fierce tussle with an old boot.

Their opinion changed when they saw the great bow wave at the end of the young man's line. An hour later the fish was still charging up and down the river but the novice – almost instinctively – knew that this fish could not be bullied in. Two hours passed and then the fish just seemed to realise the game was up. It swam straight into the net. The fish weighed a little over 40lb (18.1kg) and even the most experienced salmon fisher is unlikely in a lifetime of fishing ever to catch a fish of that size. The young man never fished again.

THE TERRIBLE CHILD

SCOTLAND, 1935

Salmon fight like the devil and are the most beautiful fish imaginable, but at times they can seem stupid to the point of suicide. Which is why many experienced fishermen are happy to admit that, in terms of the skill needed to catch them, salmon cannot be compared to trout.

The writer George Brennand, an enormously experienced game fisherman, describes a day's salmon fishing on the Tweed that illustrates the point perfectly, but it also reveals the remarkable unpredictability of fish and fishing.

Brennand was staying at a hotel in which a large number of fishermen had gathered. Most of them were middle-aged or older, but one man had brought his young son, a boy still in his early teens. When the youngster and his father arrived at the hotel some 25 excellent salmon were being laid out on the flagstones in the hall. The other fishermen had enjoyed a red-letter day, but they were aghast to hear the young man remark that salmon fishing seemed just too easy.

Among the fishermen gathered in the hall were some of the best and most experienced salmon fishers in Britain. Two of them – brothers – considered spring salmon fishing with an almost religious fervour. Their tackle was perfect and showed signs each new season that the brothers had spent virtually every day of the close season varnishing and re-varnishing their rods, oiling their reels and generally preparing with meticulous care for sport to begin again.

After the youth's remarks about salmon fishing – delivered in front of the assembled salmon fishermen in the hotel and in an extremely loud voice – a low murmur of disapproval and dark mutterings could be heard.

Later that evening in the dining room, and quite oblivious to the outraged looks of those who shared his table, the same young man continued to speak about salmon fishing as if he were a world authority. Brennand, who sat at a nearby table, was astonished that blood was not shed. The young man ended his long speech with the statement that, despite the fact that he had not caught so much as a gudgeon in all his life, he knew he would land as many fish the next day as anyone else in the hotel. He even went so far as to try to arrange a bet with one of the purple-faced old men at the other end of the table.

Dinner over, the fishermen retired to the drawing room where conversation flowed only once the young man had retired for the night.

Next morning father and son set off for the riverbank and Pot Point beat. Brennand saw no more of them until six o'clock that evening when, returning to the hotel with three good salmon, he found the hall of the hotel almost overflowing with row upon row of bigger-than-average fish. Slightly apart from the other fish there was a row of eight magnificent springers. Each fish in that row of eight was considerably bigger than any other single fish in the hall. All eight had been caught by the dreadful youth, who had never landed a fish of any species before. He had lost five more. The two brothers with half a century of experience between them returned with a total of just four fish. And throughout the rest of the week the terrible child, as he came to be known, continued to do just as well as any of the other fishermen. Brennand must have longed to take the boy for a difficult day's trout fishing and see him draw a blank.

BARBEL ON A FLY

ENGLAND, 1936

Anglers often like to make things as difficult for themselves as possible. How else can we explain the rule on some chalkstreams that dry fly is the only allowable method and that no casting is allowed unless the angler has first spotted a rising fish? How else can we explain the fact that anglers will try to fly fish in the sea for bass when spinning or using bait would be so much more productive? The love of difficulty of course stems from the oft-repeated fact that there is more to fishing than catching fish. The more difficult it is to catch your trout, the greater the satisfaction in doing what few can do well.

But the pursuit of the difficult can be taken to extremes. Dr J.C. Mottram became an enthusiast for fly fishing for barbel. That would be reasonable enough if barbel were taken every now and then on fly, but records suggest that, as a general rule, barbel simply will not take a fly. However, the records clearly did not convince Dr Mottram. He spent several seasons developing his barbel fly-fishing techniques and against all the odds he actually had some success. How on earth did he do it?

The answer is simple. Mottram was a scientist and before he tried to catch his barbel using this most unlikely method he made a careful study of his intended quarry's habits.

Dr Mottram noticed that early in the season, when barbel tend to shoal in large numbers wherever there is shallow fast water running over gravel, it was possible to trick them using a fly tied to look like a tiny minnow. Dr Mottram experimented with a number of patterns until he hit on a winning formula: after months of painstaking research and endless days on the river he landed two barbel on his fly – a fish of 4½lb (2kg) and one of 6½lb (2.7kg).

Mottram is almost certainly the only angler mad enough to fish deliberately for barbel with a fly and actually catch anything.

But the odd thing about barbel is that very large specimens are now and then caught by accident on a fly. A 16½-pounder (7.5kg) was caught in about 1880 on the Hampshire Avon by an angler fly fishing for salmon and in 1948 a fisherman on the Kennet caught a 5lb (2.3kg) barbel that had taken his fly as it floated on the surface of the river. Even among the more eccentric branches of the fishing world this dry-fly barbel fisherman did not produce a flurry of imitators. Some things are too difficult even for fishermen!

PIKE AND SALMON

CANADA, 1936

The writer G.D. Luard fished all over the UK and Canada in search of giant pike and salmon. While fishing the Great Lakes his best friend hooked a massive Great Northern pike – a cousin of our European pike. Having landed the huge fish he tried to move it so he could cradle it in his arms ready for a photograph. Stupidly, he forgot to remove the three treble hooks that had helped him land the fish. As he struggled with the slippery pike it slid out of his grasp and one of the trebles embedded itself deeply in his hand. The two men were many miles from the nearest town and there was nothing for it but to try to cut out the hooks there and then. Luard dosed his friend with half a bottle of brandy and then spent 40 minutes hacking away at his friend's hand with a razor-sharp penknife. The injured man made barely a murmur even when the knife grated on the bones of his hand. At last the hooks were removed and Luard's friend – with hardly a comment on the previous 40 minutes of agony – started to fish again. He had lost a lot of blood but other than a momentary dizziness felt perfectly fine.

That afternoon the two decided to try for a salmon and now it was Luard's turn. He quickly hooked a large salmon on a silver spoon. The fish made several terrific runs before Luard's line gave at the knot that had tied it to the eye on the spoon. Luard cursed his luck, tied on another spoon – more carefully this time – and started to fish once again.

Almost immediately he hooked another salmon, which began to rush about just as the first had done. After one particularly fierce run the salmon seem to gain massively in weight and power. Luard was baffled until the fish made a run that took it under the boat from which the two men were fishing. As the fish passed under his rod top Luard saw that it was accompanied by another salmon, but the second salmon seemed to be swimming unusually close to the first. The battle lasted another 30 minutes, but it was only in the last few moments of the fight that Luard realised that both fish were attached to his line. It was his extra careful knot and strong line that enabled him to land two very big salmon on one cast. By any standards it was an extraordinary performance, but when the two fish were in the net Luard concluded that the fish he'd hooked had run into the other salmon and in doing so the hook that held it had slipped through the eye of a spoon lodged in the other salmon's mouth. And that spoon was the very spoon he had lost in his earlier fish.

SHARK ON A LEAD
AUSTRALIA, 1936

The American writer Zane Grey fished worldwide. His stories of vicious tiger shark, giant hammerheads and spectacular marlin made him a legend in his own lifetime. In fact, after Izaak Walton he is still probably the best-known angling author in the world. But despite his fame and his experience even Grey must have been astonished at the behaviour of some of the fish he caught.

Once, while fishing off the coast of Australia, he hooked an enormous hammerhead shark. The crew of his boat instantly cleared the decks, expecting a battle of titanic proportions, for it was clear from the moment of the strike that this was a very heavy fish indeed. But without panicking Zane Grey began to play the fish in the most bizarre way. Instead of using the full power of rod and reel in an attempt to tire the shark, Grey seemed to make every effort to play it in the gentlest manner possible. He simply led it up and down as if it was a poodle out for a walk on a lead. After an hour or so the crew must have thought Grey was mad – if he continued to treat the shark as considerately as this they would still be attached to it in a week's time. What on earth was he playing at?

Still Grey continued to lead the hammerhead up and down and it was only after some time that the crew noticed that despite – or perhaps because of – his tactics, Grey had managed to bring the shark to the surface close to the boat. This was something they would have expected only if he'd fought it tooth and nail. Against all the odds the gentle treatment seemed to be working. Soon the huge fish was swimming quietly just feet from the side of the boat. Grey instructed his men to get ready with their gaffs and rope. The trick, as Grey later explained, was to lead the fish to the boat without putting any pressure on it and then get a rope round its front and back ends. By the time it realised what was going on and that it had been captured, it would be too late for the shark to do anything about it.

And that's exactly what happened with the hammerhead. It was lashed to the side of the boat and only then did it go berserk, thrashing wildly so the whole boat bucked and kicked in the water, but even a 600lb (272kg) hammerhead shark is no match for a large steel fishing boat.

Grey always maintained that this was the best way with hammerheads and other big shark species. Exerting pressure on them simply goaded them to a fury and meant several exhausting hours for the angler – hours that, as often as not, resulted in the loss of the fish anyway.

The only drawback to Grey's method was that the shark was often still full of fight when he returned to port and on at least one occasion a shark being taken up the beach caused pandemonium when it took a bite out of one of the men carrying it!

TWOSOME

WALES, 1937

The River Wye was once the greatest of English salmon rivers. Not only did it produce a lot of salmon both in the spring and the autumn, but it also produced some very big individual specimens. Being in one of the last truly rural parts of Britain the river wasn't heavily fished either – well, at least not until motorways and much wider car ownership made the river accessible to far more people. In the heady days of the 1930s this beautiful, quiet river was full of salmon and fished largely by the locals.

Very occasionally fishermen with miles of river to wander did bump into each other. Sometimes they even clashed over who should fish a particular pool first, but there is only one record, as far as anyone is aware, of two anglers sharing not just the water but the fish in it.

It happened on a glorious autumn day near Ross. Two men met at a point where both had caught fish in previous years. The anglers knew each other by sight, but theirs was just a nodding acquaintance. They had never spoken a word to each other and for reasons that will become obvious they were not likely to become the best of friends.

No one knows which of the two started to fish first, but by the time each had noticed the other they were both fishing and they were only 20–30ft (6.1–9.1m) apart. Each thought the other would do the decent thing and give way. Both carried on fishing. They were spinning and casting dangerously close to each other, but for the time being they got away with it. The frosty silence was intense. Each man knew it was absurd to pretend to ignore the other, but the moment for generosity of spirit was past and it was too late now to go back. Grimly they fished on.

Then something quite unprecedented happened. Both men hooked a salmon within seconds of each other; both seemed to be into a very good fish. Both thought that having landed their fish they would depart for the next pool and the whole embarrassing episode would be over.

But something was wrong. The two fish were fighting in an extremely odd manner. Instead of the struggles of the one making the other head off in a different direction it seemed that the two fish were determined to stay right next to each other. Then suddenly the terrible truth dawned. Both men had hooked the same fish. Their two lures must have swung right in front of the salmon's nose at precisely the same moment and, lunging at them, the hapless fish had been hooked twice.

What had started as a kind of icy stand-off was likely to end in a fist fight unless the two men could agree on who should take the salmon home. Perhaps they would share it and become fast friends. Perhaps it would get off. As the fish neared the bank the same thoughts went through both men's minds.

At the last minute and in a manner that was at least as astonishing as the whole business of hooking the same fish in the first place, both sets of hooks failed and the salmon – a good fish that probably weighed 15lb (6.8kg) – slipped away into the dark water.

If the two had spoken and joked about reaching the same pool at precisely the same moment then they would never have hooked the same salmon, but they might have become friends. As it was, locked into an enduring silence that had now lasted almost half an hour, there was no going back. With the fish gone, the men packed up in a huff and set off grumpily in different directions without a word to each other.

FISH ON TAP

UNITED STATES, 1938

Americans like to make sure that the customer is always satisfied, which may explain why fishing clubs in the States can seem most bizarre by British standards. But the long-vanished Turnstile Fishing Club in California must count as one of the strangest even by American standards.

An English visitor in the 1930s – he was a keen fisherman – remembered agreeing to visit the club because he was intrigued by his host's assurance that they could fish despite the fact that they'd just got back from a club and it was two o'clock in the morning!

'We fish whenever we like,' said his host. 'We've got it all sorted. The trout are there and the club makes sure they're always biting!'

When he arrived at the club the visitor was greeted by an official dressed like a doorman at an expensive London restaurant. His coat was ceremoniously taken and he was offered a fishing rod and a fly. He was then invited to step out on to a specially built veranda.

By this time the visiting fisherman thought he'd wandered on to a film set. All around were mounted trophies, and paintings of fish on walls that seemed to have been designed to look like an Austrian hunting lodge, yet this was a modern concrete building on the edge of an artificial lake.

Then the front of the veranda was suddenly illuminated by bright lights. Two huge doors slid open and the lake was there right in front of him. The fisherman was invited to cast and within seconds he'd caught a fish. Most casts produced a rise or a hooked fish, but then after half an hour the lights went out and the fisherman was told that was the end of his session. Just as he was leaving he was presented with his successful fly carefully mounted in a box.

'I hope it will remind you a very special and successful outing,' said the doorman as he handed the fisherman his coat.

FISH THEFT

SCOTLAND, 1938

It was almost certainly the publication of *Tarka the Otter* that marked a sea change in attitudes to the otter. For centuries it was simply accepted among country people that the only good otter was a dead one, but Henry Williamson made us realise that the otter is a very special animal indeed. And he did it just in time. By the 1960s persecution and habitat loss had reduced the English population of otters to dangerously low levels from which more recently they have happily recovered.

In Scotland, though the animal was equally disliked for eating salmon and trout – as if it should change its diet to turnips to suit its human critics – the otter had the great advantage of space. People are relatively scarce in Scotland so otters survived in far greater numbers than they did in England. Despite their often resentful attitude to otters at least one fisherman has had reason to be grateful to these much maligned animals.

The fisherman in question had had a terrible day on a remote northern spate river. He had flogged the water continually and was baffled by his lack of success. He knew the river well and had fished often, with some success, in similar conditions. But this day was turning into a nightmare.

By five o'clock he'd decided that enough was enough and he began to pack up. His rods and reels safely stowed, he began the long walk to the lodge. This took him along the bank of the river and two fields down from the last pool he'd fished he saw something both comic and out of the ordinary. A young otter was battling to pull a big salmon from the river by its tail.

The fisherman watched in astonishment for some time before realising that this could be his chance to redeem his disastrous day. He dropped his tackle on the bank and walked briskly towards the otter, which dropped the fish and ran, but only at the very last moment.

The fisherman reached the lodge an hour later with a fresh-run springer of nearly 10lb (4.5kg), but he had the decency to admit that a far better fisherman than he could ever hope to be had really caught the fish.

MISTAKEN IDENTITY

ENGLAND, 1947

H.G. Michelmore used to fish the River Dart at South Hams in Devon. It was an excellent bit of water with plenty of good free-rising trout. However, the beat he fished most regularly was part of an American firing range and practice battle-ground. Over the years numerous servicemen had been accidentally killed and one day in the late 1940s Michelmore noticed 50 or 60 yards (45.7–54.9m) from the bank a fresh mound of earth with a white cross at its head. From then on he never passed the place without bowing his head and remembering the poor soldier who had died. He felt so sad about it that he never actually wandered over to view the grave more closely.

Having served in the Great War himself Michelmore was acutely sensitive to the memory of any fallen comrade, particularly in a case like this where a young man's life had been pointlessly wasted.

After some time Michelmore found he was fishing more often in the South Hams area. He felt a great affinity with the soldier lying in his grave just a few yards from the bank and he began to salute quietly and unobtrusively whenever he passed the spot.

Then one bright summer morning Michelmore's wife decided to accompany her husband on his regular fishing trip to South Hams. This was a rare event indeed, but Michelmore was delighted to have company. As they walked together along the riverbank enjoying the warm breeze and the crisp early sun he recounted the story of the dead soldier and how deeply it had affected him. He explained that each time he passed the soldier's grave he felt strangely moved by the young man's end, but comforted himself with the thought that at least one man had not forgotten.

When they reached the place, Michelmore pointed through the trees to the barely visible white cross. His wife asked him if he was going to fish, but Michelmore explained that he did not feel comfortable fishing the place despite the fact that it was one of the best parts of the river.

'I think you might be able to from now on,' said his wife in a quiet voice.

'What on earth do you mean?' asked Michelmore.

Without a word Mrs Michelmore set off through the undergrowth towards the grave. A few minutes later she returned with what looked like a barely suppressed grin on her face.

Her husband thought the smirk was rather unwarranted, but he said nothing.

'So, what was his name?' he enquired.

'Well,' said his wife, 'he appears to have died in 1944 and his name was Officer's Latrine!'

From that day on Michelmore avoided the spot, but for very different reasons.

SATURDAY AND SUNDAY

SCOTLAND, 1948

Even as late as the 1980s a visitor to one or two areas of Scotland would have been surprised to see, in children's playgrounds every Sunday, locks on swings and roundabouts. The idea was to make sure that children were not seen in public having fun on the sabbath. Generous-hearted Presbyterians take these things very seriously indeed which is why the actions of a long-dead and long-forgotten minister of that religion will seem astonishing only to those who do not share their religious beliefs.

The minister in question was almost as fanatical about fishing as he was about religion and the strict observance of the sabbath. He had fished many places and caught huge numbers of salmon, but despite 50 years in search of a really big fish he'd never caught one over 20lb (9.1kg).

Then one summer evening he found himself fishing a small, short Highland river a day or so after heavy rain. It was a Saturday and experience told him that this was just the time to make a good bag, but this river had never produced a really big fish so thoughts of breaking the long-wished-for record were far from his mind. He fished through the afternoon and evening and as dusk fell he was pleased to note in his little fishing diary the two beautiful 10-pounders (4.5kg) that lay on the bank beside him. There was enough light for a few more casts so he decided to fish his way down the biggest pool on the river, which was little more than

30 yards (27.4m) across and 100 yards (91.4m) long, but it was deep and rocky and somehow looked very promising indeed.

A long silver flank showed as he made his first cast. Nothing. He cast again and the line came sweetly round in the current. Still nothing. One more cast and it would be too dark to fish. Out went the line and no sooner had it settled on the water than the loops of loose line the minister held in his hand began to shoot out from between his fingers. He counted slowly to three and raised his rod. The rod was almost wrenched out of his hand as a powerful fish rocketed down and across the pool.

The minister's Presbyterian convictions had not dulled his sporting instincts and having survived the shock of this first rush, he determined to bring this fish to the bank come what may. The first crisis came seconds later when the fish reached a glide on the far side of a large boulder that rose about 2ft (0.6m) out of the water halfway across the stream. By standing on tiptoe and holding his rod by the very tip of the butt he managed to keep the line clear of the obstruction. The fish, having rushed round the back of the boulder, came back to the minister's side and then swam steadily back towards the head of the pool where the water was deepest. This gave the minister time to think. He kept steady pressure on the fish, which continued doggedly to move back and forth across the head of the pool but all the time staying deep.

By this time the sun had vanished below the horizon and but for the fact that it was a clear night with a full moon the minister would long ago have lost the battle. In the ghostly blueish-white light he could just discern the more treacherous stones along the bank and would be able to avoid them if the fish again rushed downstream. This did seem most unlikely as the fish appeared quite happy to stay morosely where the tumbling waters first entered this part of the river and had, over centuries, gouged a deep, dark pool.

Then, for no apparent reason, the minister gained a little line. Almost an hour and a half had passed since the battle had commenced and the fish had clearly begun to tire. More line slowly came back to the reel. With a surge towards the opposite bank the fish rose in the water and the minister got his first sight of a salmon that was much closer to 30lb (13.6kg) than 20lb (9.1kg). If he was careful and his luck held this would be the fish of a lifetime; the long-awaited giant that had eluded him for 50 years.

The fish set off again, but this time more slowly, for the shallower bottom end of the pool; the minister followed carefully along the bank. Then, for reasons he could never in later life explain, he looked at his watch. It was 20 minutes before midnight. In 20 minutes it would be Sunday, when fishing was strictly forbidden by the minister's own church. Twenty minutes to land the fish of a lifetime. He was sure he could do it. But what if his watch showed 12 o'clock and the fish had still not been beaten?

What would he do then? He dismissed the terrible consequences of this possibility from his mind and put as much pressure as he dared on his line. With a sinking heart the minister somehow sensed that this very fresh fish had got a second wind and that it would therefore be very difficult to defeat before midnight.

He had followed the salmon to the very limit of the pool. It would have to cross extremely shallow water to go below and was unlikely to do so. Another powerful run and the fish was nearing that dangerous boulder. The minister, arms and back aching almost unendurably, looked again at his watch. Five minutes to 12. The seconds ticked away. Twice the fish came so close that an experienced gillie might have had a chance of netting it, but the minister always fished alone. Then the minister looked down again at his watch and saw that it was midnight. He knew what he had to do. When the fish began again to move down the pool the minister refused to give line or to move. His rod creaked as it bent into the powerful fish. Then, with a sharp crack like a rifle shot, the line parted and the biggest fish the minister had ever hooked vanished for ever. Given another half an hour he would almost certainly have landed the fish, but for the sake of his religious beliefs he had deliberately lost the fish of a lifetime.

It was Sunday and as the minister walked sadly up to the road he comforted himself that he had at least obeyed the dictates of his conscience, but he was never again to hook such a big fish and he died a few years later a disappointed man.

BIRD MEETS FISH

ENGLAND, 1950

It is reasonably common to find two pike have died while trying to swallow each other. Twenty-pound (9.1kg) pike have been found locked together like this as well as pike weighing just a few ounces. These ferocious creatures are sometimes undone by their very fearlessness. Pike have hundreds of teeth that point down towards the throat, so having grabbed something too big to swallow the pike cannot eject it and chokes to death. Meanwhile, of course, the other pike – the one that was meant to be swallowed – dies because it cannot withdraw its head.

In fact, pike have been found dead with all sorts of odd things stuck in their gullets – and all because of those backward-pointing teeth. One of the oddest pike deaths came in a large Kentish lake normally considered a trout fishery. A swan was spotted drifting apparently lifeless up against a reed bank. The local water bailiff rowed out to see if he could retrieve the swan. He reached the bird and leaned over to take it out of the water. Now a swan is a very big bird indeed, but this was ridiculous. He couldn't lift it from the water. He reached round, grabbed the bird's neck and tried to raise its head. As he lifted the neck a massive pike loomed up through the water. For a split second the bailiff thought the fearsome-looking fish was still alive, but like the swan it was stone dead.

Back at the fishing lodge the pike's teeth had to be prised off the swan's head with a chisel. The giant fish had obviously glimpsed the swan's head underwater as the bird fed on weeds and other aquatic bits and pieces. The fish had clearly decided this was something edible. Having lunged forward and got the swan's head and part of its neck into its gullet there was no going back. But of course even a 25lb (11.3kg) pike was never going to be able to eat the rest of the massive bird. The pike choked to death or drowned because it could no longer breathe through its gills. With its head stuck in the pike's mouth the swan too had no chance.

THE LADY'S FISH
IRELAND, 1952

Husbands and their wives have often taken up fishing together, or one partner takes up the sport soon after discovering that the other is a fisher simply to avoid becoming a fishing widow or – more rarely – widower. It is a sad fact, but a fact nonetheless, that men are far more likely to give up their wives than their fishing. Occasionally a couple develop an equivalent enthusiasm for the sport and this can have unexpected consequences.

Mr and Mrs Williams, a couple who fished together in Ireland every summer, found that as the years wore on they were becoming more and more alike in their fishing habits. If they went off separately in the morning they would discover when they met again at lunchtime that they had fished with the same three flies that morning and that they had changed their flies at pretty much the same time. If one caught a brace of trout it was as likely as not that the other would also catch a brace. But their most extraordinary exploit came on a blustery day when they were fishing a famous Irish lough known both for its good salmon and for numerous big trout.

Their gillie and boatman was one of the most experienced on the lough and the couple were happy to fish wherever he suggested. They tried the eastern shore. As the boat drifted along parallel to the bank and about 300 yards (274m) offshore the first rise of the day turned out to be a really big fish. It was hooked by Mrs Williams. At first she thought it must be a salmon, but the gillie insisted it was almost certainly a very large trout. She played her fish carefully – perhaps too carefully – but the blustery conditions made things difficult. The fish went deep, ran quickly and then cartwheeled into the air, landing with a terrifying splash. Each time this happened – and it happened again and again – Mrs Williams was convinced that when she reeled in the slack line her fish would be gone, but her luck held and it stayed on, but still full of fight. Ten minutes passed like this and the fish – which the gillie estimated at about 12lb (5.4kg) – suddenly decided it would charge towards their boat. Mrs Williams just about managed to keep in touch and the gillie began to think that this fish might indeed be landed.

Then the boat rose on a particularly big wave at precisely the moment that the fish chose to come to the surface on the next wave ahead of the boat. As the fish slid down the back of its wave with the whole weight of the water pressing on it the line gave at the hook knot.

Mrs Williams said nothing. She lit a cigarette and asked to be put ashore. She told her husband to fish on without her. He knew better than to offer any words of comfort – the fish of a lifetime had been lost and nothing he could say would do any good. He left his wife on the bank knowing that she would deal with this tragedy in the way that suited her best. She asked for an hour and her husband agreed, telling her that he would fish the same drift again before returning to pick her up.

The gillie rowed into position and Mr Williams began fishing again, but more to soothe his shattered nerves than in any real hope of a fish. Ten minutes later and about half a mile (800m) downwind of poor Mrs Williams, Mr Williams rose another tremendous fish. The take was particularly exciting as the fly was almost out of the water when a huge mouth broke the waves and gulped it down.

'It was as if I was attached to Moby Dick,' said Williams later. The fish tore off 100 yards (91.4m) of line with ease, but then something very strange happened. The great powerful fish simply gave up the ghost. Williams was convinced it was a trick. As he reeled in, keeping steady pressure on the fish, he every minute expected a sudden rush, a leap into the air – anything to match the force of that first run. But instead the fish came to the boat as if it was quite happy to be captured. As soon as the gillie lifted the net from the water both men knew that they were never likely again to see such a splendid specimen. It was in the peak of condition – long, powerful and beautifully marked. It later weighed in at precisely 11¼lb (5.1kg). So why had it given up so quickly? The answer wasn't hard to find.

When the gillie went to unhook the fish, there in the side of its mouth was Mrs Williams's fly! Her long battle had almost exhausted the great fish which is why, when her husband hooked it, it had only one run left in it.

In over 40 years on the lough the gillie had never seen anything like this before. Mr Williams was astonished and he asked the gillie to row immediately back to Mrs Williams. To her credit she was as delighted by the capture of her fish as she was astonished to find it in the boat. She consoled herself with the thought that she had played the fish while her husband had really only landed it. That was the only possible explanation for the almost instant capitulation of such a magnificent fish.

A BRIDGE TOO FAR

ENGLAND, 1954

A fanatical coarse fisherman had long wanted to buy a house by his favourite river, the Thames. At last the chance came and he bought a small cottage with a long garden running down to the river. He then bought a small boat and began to prepare for the opening of the coarse fishing season. He cleaned his rods and reels, sharpened his hooks, checked the meshes of his landing net and did everything possible to ensure that his life by the river started in the way he meant it to continue.

On his inaugural outing he decided to fish a few hundred yards above a weir. It was an area of the river known for its big pike and if there was one species this fisherman loved catching above all others it was pike. He'd caught his first pike – a lively 6-pounder (7.3kg) – when he was just ten, and now 40 years later he wanted to celebrate the acquisition of his dream house by landing a pike over 10lb (4.5kg).

On 16 June, the opening day of the season, he got up at dawn, prepared sandwiches and a large flask of hot tea, checked his tackle one last time and walked proudly to the end of his garden. His new boat was bobbing happily in the current and he loaded his tackle aboard and set off. The weir was about half a mile (800m) downstream, but the river was running quickly and it took just ten minutes to reach the chosen spot.

He threw out his anchor, set up his best pike rod and cast

a large sprat into an area of slack water just a little to the side of the main current. On his first cast the float vanished and a good pike was soon engaged in a fierce tussle at the end of the line. It was an 8-pounder (3.6kg), not quite the hoped-for double-figure fish but a good start nonetheless.

According to the newspaper reports that later appeared, it was at this point that everything started to go wrong. As the fisherman tried to unhook his pike, he slipped over backwards and was lucky not to have fallen into the river. The downside of the tumble was that the pike fell on the fisherman's face and sank its teeth into his nose. The fish's sharp teeth had only a slight hold on the skin, but in an unthinking reaction to the pain the fisherman yanked the fish away, leaving a nasty wound that immediately began to bleed. Trying to keep his temper despite the pain and the blood now dripping freely on to his shirt the fisherman gently returned the pike to the water and took stock of his situation.

As he stood dabbing his nose and wondering whether or not to call it a day he noticed that his home-made anchor – a chunk of concrete with a steel ring through it – had come adrift and his boat was slipping rapidly downstream. The fisherman lunged for his oars, but one had already slipped overboard. What on earth was he to do? The boat had picked up speed as the water began to race towards the weir and he suddenly realised that in a few moments his idyllic trip had turned into a nightmare. If he couldn't stop the boat before it reached the weir he might even be killed. He tried using the remaining oar as a paddle but it had little effect against the power of the current. He glanced back to the security of the bank, but there was not a soul to be seen. He shouted for help, but no reply came. The few houses he passed seemed deserted and he began to panic. He tried to steer the boat away from the main current, but without success and then, looking over his shoulder, he realised that the boat was now only a hundred yards from the foaming waters of the weir. Just before the weir itself there was narrow wooden footbridge, but there was no way the fisherman could jump from the boat and reach it as he passed underneath.

Then he had an idea. It was a long shot but it might just work. He quickly attached his heaviest wire trace to his line, added four large treble hooks and a weight and sat down to wait for the boat to reach the bridge. He had just one chance but he was ready. At the moment the boat cleared the bridge the fisherman expertly cast his weight and hook back at it. The weight went high over the bridge and landed in the water on the upstream side. The fisherman, his boat still moving downstream, reeled in as fast as he could and as the weight and hooks were dragged back over the footbridge they caught in the bridge's wire superstructure. The fisherman turned side-on to the bridge and gradually allowed his rod to take the strain. The rod bent into a hoop and the line sang in the breeze, but the boat began to slow and the line held. If the fisherman had decided to try for pretty much any species other than pike that day, his tackle would not have been strong enough to hold the rowing boat in the current. But the pike tackle was powerful and the hooks held until someone crossing the bridge a little later noticed that the man standing in a boat in the middle of the river and apparently fishing for a footbridge was actually in serious trouble. The police were called and a motor launch rescued the fisherman just as his line finally gave way.

TOO EASY

SCOTLAND, 1955

Game fishermen will never admit it, but every now and then the mighty salmon – the ultimate quarry of the freshwater angler – behaves like the stupidest stickleback. When conditions are perfect, with just the right amount of water and just the right temperature, salmon will virtually throw themselves on the bank. A situation like this is very rare indeed but it does happen, which is why the cost of salmon fishing increases so dramatically for certain weeks of the year on certain rivers. You still need a great deal of skill to land your salmon wherever and whenever you hook it, but record books always reveal the best weeks and by best weeks people mean those times at which the maximum number of taking fish are in the water.

One angler who experienced a day when the salmon were almost literally throwing themselves out of the river was Lord Hardinge of Penshurst. He was fishing the Helmsdale in the time before high-seas netting drastically reduced the numbers of salmon entering British rivers. On the day in question the beat allotted to him – the beat below the falls – was absolutely crammed with fish, but there was no sign that they were in a taking mood.

At 10a.m. Hardinge began to fish. After half an hour he made a long cast and immediately saw a large V-shape bow-wave caused by a fish shooting across the river to grab his barely sunk fly. Minutes later the first fish of the day was on the bank. Despite decades of regular fishing Hardinge had never seen anything like this before. But more was to follow, for something had got into those salmon and, as Hardinge himself admitted, they would have taken absolutely anything however badly presented.

After the first salmon had been landed Hardinge cast to the same spot and precisely the same thing happened – a huge bow-wave chased the departing fly across the pool and devoured it. Within 40 minutes he had hooked and played four big salmon from the same spot on four consecutive casts. Only one of them got off, but as Hardinge said afterwards, if another fisherman had been there, the total of fish for those 40 minutes would have been eight fish. The only problem was how fast you could land them – it was as easy as netting them, but then, for some indefinable reason, the frenzy ended as quickly as it had begun. Never again was such a thing to happen to Hardinge and he never heard of it happening to any other angler.

UMBRELLA MENACE

SCOTLAND, 1955

Poaching is always a problem. It can take many forms, from the harmless attempt of a child to hook a trout on a worm and a bent pin to murderous high-seas netting that may destroy a complete river system's salmon stocks in a few years or even months. Individual poachers also vary enormously, from the small-time village poacher to the commercial gang bent on wholesale slaughter. Every now and then a poacher of extraordinary eccentricity pops up. One such was an elderly woman – it was thought that she was a local retired schoolteacher of the greatest apparent respectability but with an inordinate passion for fish. She operated on the falls of a small spate river near her home. Whenever the river was up and the salmon were running she was always to be seen watching intently from a position about two-thirds of the way up the falls and off to the side. She never stood on the bridge higher up, but always on the footpath. For years, whenever she was seen in her favourite spot it was assumed that she was out on one of her nature rambles and simply hoped to catch a glimpse of a salmon launching itself into the air to clear the narrow falls and reach the pool above. So few people paid much attention to the fact that she always carried a large and curiously heavy-looking umbrella on her walks. True, it was often raining while she stood in apparent contemplation overlooking the river, but it was only much later that people remembered that, curiously, the umbrella never seemed to be open and in use.

Then one fateful morning the real purpose of the old lady's river watching was discovered. For her the discovery was sheer bad luck; for the other villagers it became a local legend that was talked about for years afterwards. A newcomer to the village who happened to be a keen fisherman was out a little earlier than usual and decided to walk up the river to see if anything was happening. It had rained overnight and there was, he thought, a good chance that the salmon would be moving. The old lady was there before him. Having lived in the village all her life she knew pretty much the habits of all the locals. None would be out so early for a walk. As he reached the bridge above the falls the newcomer saw out of the corner of his eye an elderly woman he had noticed often around the village. He was about to shout 'Good morning' when what he witnessed left him completely speechless. Something silver flashed for an instant in front of the old lady and in that split second her arm, which had been holding a long, unopened umbrella aloft, came down in a flash, knocking the silver object, obviously a salmon, out of its path. The newcomer moved quietly into a position that would give him a clearer view of what was going on. As he did so he saw the old woman leap like a girl of 20 down the steep bank and, using the handle of her umbrella, she pulled out an apparently dead, but perfectly fresh salmon. The newcomer was afraid the old lady would spot him so, rather than go any further on his walk, he retraced his steps back to the village, but resolved to investigate this business further.

Over the following three months he saw the old lady several times in her chosen place, apparently innocently watching the falls, but she always happened to be there just after fresh rain and each time he watched her he saw that umbrella put to deadly use. The thing that he found most astonishing was the old woman's speed and strength. She was quite clearly so experienced that she could time her blow exactly to coincide with the salmon's leap. Admittedly the river was so narrow at the falls that you could virtually jump it, but a leaping salmon is poised in mid-air only for an instant. For the old woman that was enough – no sooner was the salmon in the air than down came her umbrella with a mighty thump. The salmon crashed back into the river and she scooped it out in the calmer waters below. In an average year the old woman probably did little harm, but what she was doing was illegal. The newcomer was in a difficult position. He didn't want to make himself extremely unpopular in the village by going to the police, but he thought she ought to stop. After much deliberation he decided that the best plan would be to mention to someone, anyone in the village who was known as a gossip, that a group of schoolchildren had been inventing a ridiculous story about people poaching salmon on the local river using a strange new gaff.

Within weeks of setting the rumour going the newcomer noticed that the old lady no longer appeared at the falls and the salmon were left in peace to leap and soar free of the risk of meeting a rolled umbrella halfway to the top.

BODY COUNT
ENGLAND, 1956

Rivers are dangerous places and every year they claim many lives, which may explain the curious fact that in terms of the number of deaths per year fishing is one of our most dangerous sports. Fishing can also be a rather spooky business, particularly when one is fishing some remote lake or stream with the mists of evening rolling in across the fields. Perhaps it is at times like this that stories of spectres and inexplicable events are born.

One such story has a ghostly feel to it, but it happened on a sunny day in June on the River Thames just a few miles from London. A boy fishing with his father was astonished to see what looked like a body floating past him as he fished for roach on a wide bend in the river. He called to his father and the two of them quickly waded out to the dark object. It was indeed a body. The father, worried that his son would be deeply upset, told him to run along the riverbank to the nearest house which was 300–400 yards (274–366m) away.

'I'll try to revive her,' he shouted as his son disappeared from view. But he knew that the young girl he was now dragging towards the shallows was beyond all help. Despite his misgivings the fisherman did his best to empty the girl's lungs and bring her back to life. The fisherman had some knowledge of first aid and the girl, though completely lifeless and white as a sheet, had clearly not been in the river for long. He tried mouth-to-mouth resuscitation for what seemed like an age but, as he'd feared, there was no response. Then he noticed something very odd. The girl was dressed in remarkably old-fashioned clothes. A crumpled black bonnet still dangled from a ribbon round her neck. She wore a long black dress and a tight bodice laced at the back.

'Probably got drunk at a fancy dress party on a boat and fell in, poor girl,' thought the fisherman. 'Why on earth don't people notice when these things happen?' he wondered. Then with a pang he noticed how extraordinarily beautiful the girl was. Though very pale she had the most delicate features and a skin that, in life, would have appeared flawless.

In the next instant his son returned and the fisherman told him there was no hope. By this time a small crowd had gathered, but the fisherman and his son sat some way from the body feeling helpless and waiting for the police to arrive. Within an hour the body had been taken away, the fisherman and his son had been interviewed and the crowd had dispersed. It was too depressing now to bother about fishing so father and son set off on the long walk to the car park.

In the days following the discovery of the body the fisherman scanned the local newspaper for news of the drowning. He hoped he wasn't being ghoulish but he couldn't get the memory of the girl out of his mind and somehow, discovering her name and something about who she was might, he felt, make some sense of the whole thing. The days passed and turned into weeks. Having scoured the papers and found nothing he assumed it must have been given a small space somewhere and that he'd missed it. He went over the papers as if his life depended on it. Still nothing. He telephoned several local papers and gave the news editors brief details of what had happened and when. In each case he was told that the paper had received no story even remotely fitting the description. The fisherman was baffled. A month had gone by and the only thing he could think of doing was to contact the local police. He rang the nearest police station and explained who he was. The officer he spoke to said the story didn't immediately ring any bells but that he would call back.

Half an hour later the phone rang. 'We have no record of a girl drowning in the river.'

The fisherman was astonished and asked if it was possible that the girl in the river had been dealt with by another police station.

'No. Not possible,' said the policeman. 'All records for the police in this area are held centrally and we wouldn't have missed something as serious as a body in the river. We might spend months trying to identify it and there would have to be an inquest. I can tell you that it really didn't happen – you must have imagined it.'

The fisherman gave up, but for months afterwards he thought about the girl in the river. Whenever she drifted into his thoughts he saw her pale beautiful face, but as time passed he began to wonder if it had happened at all.

On Christmas day two years after he found the girl in the river, the fisherman unwrapped a book about London that had been published in the 1930s. It described many of the most important buildings in and around the capital. As he skimmed through it his eye caught an account of a private asylum which, according to the author, had been set up to look after girls 'from good homes' suffering from some kind of mental instability. The hospital or asylum had been just downstream of the spot at which the fisherman had found the dead girl and he immediately wondered if the girl in the river had been a patient at the hospital. Perhaps she was the daughter of someone important and her death had been kept quiet.

The fisherman decided to investigate. He quickly discovered that the asylum had closed a few years earlier, but its records were still to be found at the National

Records Office. He took a week off work and spent long hours searching through the dusty, long-forgotten files. At last in an entry for 1910 he found a faded black and white photograph of a fair-haired girl in her teens. His hand shook as he read the accompanying notes. Her name was Alice Wildman and she had gone missing one day and been found drowned in the river. The fisherman decided that it must be a coincidence or his mind was simply playing tricks – it wasn't the best of photographs and he was probably mistaken. But then he noticed something that made his hair stand on end: the date the girl had been found dead all those years ago was 18 June. He'd found the girl in the river on 18 June.

Perhaps it was all just a curious coincidence, but the fisherman never referred to the incident again and he was never able to find out any more about the girl in the river or about Alice Wildman.

DEAD CERT

ENGLAND, 1957

If you ask a doctor why fishing is like sex he is liable to explain that the excitement of fishing, like the excitement of sex, kills more middle-aged men than pretty much anything else.

There are many tales of elderly men dropping dead on the riverbank or being found looking happy but without a spark of life and adrift in a fishing boat. Many fishermen have said that when they go they'd like to go while fishing, but most would agree that even that would depend on the exact circumstances.

One elderly fisherman on the Avon had spent most of his adult life in pursuit of a really big barbel. He'd caught dozens weighing around 8–9lb (3.6–4.1kg) but that double-figure fish looked set to elude him until the end.

The old man put in many hours and few could question his skill. It was just that somehow luck was never with him when he needed it. Then came the day of reckoning. He was fishing a bunch of lobworms in a fast glide that had produced several notable barbel in the past. After re-baiting he'd cast out and hardly had the bait settled on the bottom than a deep, strong pull had the old man leaping for his rod like a 20-year-old. He played the fish as if his life depended on it and after almost a quarter of an hour a barbel that must have weighed at least 12lb (5.4kg) turned on its side and admitted defeat. The old man never fished alone and his companion, who was also in his seventies, got ready to net the monster.

Just as the barbel cleared the rim of the net the old man announced: 'Well, if I die now I'll die a happy man.' And in that very instant, to the utter astonishment of his friend, he pitched forward into the river and, as the doctor later said, was very probably dead before he hit the water. The fish weighed exactly 12lb 6oz (5.6kg) and it was returned alive to the river exactly where the old man had breathed his last.

DEFINITELY NO MACKEREL

ENGLAND, 1957

A small sailing boat with two fishermen aboard set out for a day in pursuit of mackerel just 1 mile (1.6km) or so off the coast. It was a bright sunny day, with a light swell and just enough wind to take their 12ft (3.7m) boat out to a mark they'd fished before with some success. But today the fish were simply not to be found.

The fishermen tied on the bright feathers that normally prove so deadly with mackerel and fished hard for two hours. Not a single fish of any species took the bait. They moved a little further along the coast. Still nothing. They kept an eye out for flocks of gulls massing above the water – a sure sign that mackerel are about. Nothing. The day wore on and, just as they were about to give up, one of the rods whipped over into a satisfying hoop. But this was no mackerel. The two fishermen were highly experienced and the man in touch with the fish quickly realised that whatever he had hooked was going to take a very long time to subdue.

Luckily he was using a massive old reel with nearly 600 yards (549m) of strong line and a rod as thick as a man's finger. He was unlikely to be broken, they were in a very small boat and evening was coming on – what on earth were they to do? They hated the idea of deliberately breaking the line, but it would be dark soon and their lives would be in real danger if the weather turned. Time passed while they tried to make a decision and then the decision was made for them. The great orange disc of the sun vanished and the coastline was visible only as a series of faint twinkling lights.

Two hours went by and still no sign of the fish. It kept up a dogged battle, staying close to the bottom and only now and then making a run for it. Each run was unusual, the two were later to say, in that there was no sense of panic. The fish merely stepped up its pace and line would slip from the reel steadily at first but gradually increasing in speed. Once one of these runs had begun it could not be stopped. Eventually, exhausted by the constant loss and then regaining of line, the two fisherman began to pass the rod back and forth between them. That way at least they had time to recover from the intense arm ache that playing a heavy fish quickly induces.

Another hour ticked past. By this time they were trying to follow the fish rather than trying to regain line after each run. When it made a move they sailed after it, but all the while keeping up a steady pressure.

At one stage, some three hours into the proceedings, both men began to think that they might be better off cutting their line simply because whatever was down there was probably too big for two men to handle in a small boat anyway. It was one of those rare occasions when the fisherman is actually slightly afraid of what he might find at the end of his line.

The little boat was moving through the water at quite a pace when the two men noticed that they had covered many miles from their original position. In short they had no idea where they were. As the night wore on the two men grew rather afraid. They were stuck in a small boat miles out to sea in the dark and attached to a fish that was probably too big to get in the boat. By now they were very cold.

They tried everything they could think of to throw the fish off course or at least to get it to move in another direction or show some sign that hours of pressure were beginning to weaken it. Nothing made the slightest difference. The pattern of accelerating runs followed by a short pause continued. At last, and despite the fact that they had taken turns playing the fish, they had to give up. While one held the rod the other opened his pocket knife and cut the line. They sank into the well of the boat too worn out even to speak. The sea was running quickly now and it took a further two hours to reach land. Soon after pulling their boat up the beach they made an extraordinary discovery. The giant fish, combined with wind and tide, had driven them more than 50 miles (80.5km) from home.

Two years after their tussle with the giant, unbeatable fish one of the two men was glancing through a local newspaper when he came across a curious story. A small submarine had been detected by Royal Navy patrols a few miles off the coast. The crew had tried to identify the submarine and contact its crew but without success. The submarine was detected late in the evening moving along parallel with the coast, but 20 minutes after it had been detected, the submarine – if that is what it was – disappeared from the radar screen. The following night the Navy patrols detected a similar underwater vessel and again, having been tracked for some 20 minutes, it vanished. A Navy spokesman told the newspaper reporter that they were baffled but would continue to investigate. The map that accompanied the story showed the probable route of the mystery submarine. It was further out from the coast than the two men had been that night but the course it had taken matched exactly that of the huge unstoppable fish. Had they been attached to a submarine all that time? It would certainly explain the long, fruitless battle with a fish that was bigger than anything that had ever been heard of in that region.

The fish could have been that submarine or a giant shark that had strayed into British waters. But the mystery was never solved and the submarine was never again detected.

STONE THROWING

ENGLAND, 1958

Two schoolboys who had fished together for years seldom had much luck. They were too poor to pay for train tickets to fish out of town, but they were very keen so they fished the tidal Thames near their homes in east London. At this time the Thames was still a very dirty river and it must have seemed a real achievement when, occasionally, they managed to land an eel or some other hardy fish that had braved the brackish water.

But the two boys were never bored. The place where they chose to fish was an old bomb-site still littered with the debris from an old warehouse that had been razed to the ground by German bombs. The rubble petered out at the water's edge. The warehouse cellars provided places to hide and to explore when the fish weren't biting – which was most of the time – and the boys sometimes tried to make a boat or a raft from the masses of old tins and pieces of scrap timber that lay strewn about. The friends were said to be inseparable and certainly for as long as they could remember they had played together. When one found some heavy old sea-fishing tackle in his grandfather's shed they shared it on numerous outings to the river. They collected old bottles and rags to sell to raise the money to buy hooks and nylon line. Then came triumph and disaster in one day.

It was a misty summer morning and the river still looked much as it might have looked in the nineteenth century with those warehouses that had survived the war still unrestored and smoke-blackened. They reached their favourite spot and, taking turns to cast, began to fish. Like most youngsters they were impatient and tended to reel in every five minutes to check that their bait was still on the hook. But on this day they were in luck. Within an hour they had caught half a dozen eels, a large flatfish they thought was probably a flounder and a silvery fish that could, as far as they were concerned, have been anything from a herring to a salmon.

Then, in a moment of madness when the fish had ceased to bite, one of the boys suggested they play war games. It seemed a good idea and they dashed about the piles of rubble pretending to shoot at each other. Then, inexplicably, they began to throw rocks. They didn't throw them directly at each other, but lobbed them up in the air, pretending that they were shells being hurled across the trenches. At first it was fun to dodge the incoming rocks. They were big and easy to see and as they were being tossed up high it was easy to avoid them.

Then, in the way these things happen when games get out of hand, one of the boys was hit on the head by a falling rock. His friend saw the almost casual way that his friend's knees buckled. It all seemed so slow that he almost thought his friend was adding to the game by playing at being dead. But when he ran down to check that he was all right he found that his best friend could not be woken. Twenty minutes later the distraught boy had summoned help, but nothing could be done. The boy died in hospital and his friend never went fishing again.

CHANCE IN A MILLION

ENGLAND, 1960

The gillie at Broadlands Estate in Hampshire was fishing the river with a client. They hooked what was quite clearly a huge salmon in Webb's Pool. Half an hour into the fight they had still not seen the fish. It ploughed up and down the river for what seemed like an eternity, always deep and seemingly inexhaustible. Then, in one quite uncontrollable rush, the salmon tore under the downstream bridge. The two men rushed after it and were about to pass the rod from one to another under the bridge when the line caught on the stonework and parted.

Three days later the gillie was making his usual rounds when he saw a length of line in the shallows. He recognised it as the line that had parted on the bridge during that epic battle a few days earlier. In an instant he had set up another rod, tied his line to the line trailing in the water and, hardly daring to believe his luck, he was suddenly attached once again to the giant salmon.

Unfortunately the salmon had fully recovered from its earlier tussle and was not having any of it. The gillie stayed in contention for some 20 minutes before a savage lunge broke the nylon as if it had been mere cotton.

The gillie, who had worked on the river for many years, estimated that if the fish had been landed it would have broken all records on the river.

NATURIST

ENGLAND, 1960

An elderly fisherman who'd been a member of a well-known trout fishing club for many years, used regularly to fall into the river in summer. The gillie thought he sometimes did it deliberately to cool off, but the old man insisted each time it happened that he had been trying to cast round an old willow or into a difficult corner on the far side of the stream. In doing so he had lost his balance and taken a ducking. The duckings became more frequent and the gillie and other club officials became concerned that the elderly member – he was in his eighties – might catch pneumonia. Then one very hot day in June the gillie was doing his rounds and he discovered that the elderly member had fallen in, but rather than hide in his car until his clothes dried – which is what he usually did – he'd simply carried on fishing, but without a stitch of clothing on.

Now the gillie wouldn't normally have worried much about this – club members were notoriously eccentric – but round the next bend was the local MP's wife who was also a prominent member of the local Methodist church.

The gillie was aghast. He was sure he would be held responsible if the MP's wife were confronted by this naked apparition. He remonstrated with the elderly member, who dismissed his fears with a wave.

'Nothing she hasn't seen before. Besides, she'll be moving along well ahead of me.' The gillie was horrified, but he could hardly insist. Then he had a brainwave. He wandered off for ten minutes and then returned to the still stark-naked fisherman.

'I've just seen a very big old trout under that pile of roots back the way you've come. I think he'd take a small black fly. He's a very big fish too. One of the best in the river.'

'Oh him. I've tried him several times. Can't get a fly over him at all,' came the reply.

'I think I may have the solution to that problem,' said the gillie.

The old man, who was greedy for glory and well knew the reputation of the fish under the roots, was now listening intently.

'Yes, I think I have the answer. I have an old inner tube from a lorry tyre that you could float down past the fish in. If we set you off on this bank, you can use your hand to paddle the thing within range and then it's an easy cast.'

The old man took the bait and the gillie was soon lowering him into the rubber ring which settled under his armpits.

'Told you there was a lot to be said for fishing without clothes,' said the old man.

The gillie pushed him off and watched him sail away downstream, gradually moving towards the middle of the river. He had a few casts over the trout under the roots but failed to make contact. He shouted to the gillie, but the gillie was nowhere to be seen. A few moments later the MP's wife was astonished at the sight of an elderly gentleman in a floating rubber ring gently drifting past her. All she could see was his head and as he passed he doffed his hat to her. Meanwhile, the gillie had decided that he would rescue the old man about half a mile (800m) downstream by which time he knew it would be time to pack up for the day and the MP's wife, astonished but not morally outraged, would have set off for home.

But now there was the problem of a very angry and very senior fisherman to deal with. The gillie caught the old man as he passed under a low bridge five meadows downstream. Expecting volleys of abuse, the gillie was astonished when the old man smiled and waved.

'You're a genius. Putting me in this thing was splendid. Haven't had so much fun in a long time and look!'

With that he held up three very big trout.

For years afterwards the gillie dined out on the story of the old man in the rubber ring. It was a satisfactory end to a difficult day, but it left him with one headache. Every time the elderly member came to fish he asked if he could use the rubber ring. Which was a pity as the gillie had to explain to him that some vandal had stuck a knife in it.

GIANT EEL

ENGLAND, 1964

The dangers of freshwater fishing are as nothing compared
to the dangers of the sea. On the riverbank a sudden spate
may catch the angler unawares, but on the high seas storm
and tempest can drown even the most rugged boat. Then
there are the fish themselves. No freshwater lake or river
in the world has anything to compare with the moray eel or
the great white shark for ferocity. Both species occasionally
take the unwary angler's bait but no angler in his right mind
would dream of actually trying to land either of these species.
A hooked great white will as likely as not attack the angler's
boat; a moray eel, murderous and extremely difficult to kill,
will attack the occupants of a boat if it is brought on board.
An experienced angler who sees a moray eel coming up from
the depths on the end of his line will invariably cut it free.
Luckily neither of these species is likely to trouble the angler
fishing British waters. But other horrors lie in wait in the
depths of our apparently more placid seas.

While fishing above a sunken ship some 30 miles (48.3km)
out from Poole in Dorset a fisherman hooked something
enormously powerful. This fisherman knew what he was
doing. He knew that wrecks tend to produce conger eels
because these secretive fish love to hole up in the rusted
and tangled sanctuaries created by sunken ships. The
fisherman had caught a number of very big conger eels in
the past, but this one felt like the mother of them all.

An hour after the battle began, the fisherman was still getting nowhere. Probably the great eel had wound its long tail around part of the superstructure of the wreck and it would be very difficult to budge it. But two hours later, just as the fisherman was thinking he would have to pass the rod to one of his companions – and thus lose all chance of securing a new record – the creature moved. After that the war was effectively won for even the biggest conger eel is a relatively poor fighter once it's been drawn out of the safety of a wreck.

Slowly the eel came towards the surface. The fisherman's arms were aching but he was convinced this was a new British record and he was determined to land it unaided. The other anglers on board the small fishing boat had long ago reeled in to avoid any risk that their lines might get caught up in the fray. They were peering over the side where the fisherman's 80-pound nylon vanished into the depths. Then they saw it. At first just a shimmering white mass, then a vast head with the huge mouth gaping.

'Christ! It's huge,' shouted one of the men. Normally they released unharmed any fish they caught, but this conger was so big that it would have to be gaffed simply to keep it under control when it came over the side of the boat. As luck would have it their fishing boat was about the smallest allowed for wreck fishing. It was barely 30ft (9.1m) long, old-fashioned in style and timber-built. It had a tiny wheelhouse amidships and that was just about the only cover if the weather turned nasty. But the four friends fishing together on the day they hooked the giant eel had used the boat successfully and without mishap for many years.

The fisherman fighting the eel was very experienced, as were his friends. He knew that to be safe he would have to make sure the eel was absolutely exhausted before there was any attempt to gaff it and bring it aboard. So he waited. The eel, by now on the surface, began to roll over again and again – a sure sign that the battle was well and truly over.

The skipper waited with the gaff. As soon as he had it in the fish one of the other fishermen added his gaff and the two men began to drag the fish over the gunwales. All went well, despite the eel's huge weight, until it hit the deck. At that precise moment the giant eel went berserk. It began to thrash powerfully from side to side while snapping at anything and everything within reach. The four men leapt out of the way just in time to avoid serious injury. They ran to one end of the boat, leaving the eel flailing and twisting at the other end. In its first few convulsions the eel had smashed the handles of both gaffs. Then, as it slid around with the movement of the boat on the waves, it reached the wheelhouse and with a massive blow it smashed one side of it beyond repair. Splintered wood lay everywhere; the wheelhouse was badly damaged and all the while the giant eel continued to bite and lunge and writhe. One or other of the men ran in occasionally and tried to hit it with a heavy lead-loaded club, but nothing had any effect. They fired a flare at it, but missed and burnt a hole in the side of the boat.

The eel seemed to be losing strength, but it was a full two hours before they risked going near it. It was getting dark and they would be missed if they couldn't get to the wheelhouse quickly and radio their position. They decided on a very dangerous manoeuvre – all four of them would rush the fish and quickly tip it back over the side. With the boat already damaged they could not take any further risks. It might already be very difficult to get back safely to port.

The plan worked and the now quiet fish was heaved overboard without further misadventure. One of the fishermen said later that when the eel hit the water he was convinced that it didn't drift down through the water like something dead, but that it swam strongly away. It was as if, having shown the fishermen the havoc it could wreak, it gave them the chance to put it back while they still could.

When the damaged boat limped into port the fishermen were grateful to have survived. The loss of what had certainly been a new British record fish seemed a small price to pay.

RETRIEVER

ENGLAND, 1964

Romney Marsh is one of the loneliest, most windswept regions of Britain. Here sheep have grazed for more than a thousand years and along the many drainage channels, creeks and inlets smugglers once brought their contraband ashore. But Romney Marsh is also an excellent place for the pike fisher. Here miles of water are home to some of the best pike in Britain. They grow fat on the teeming roach and rudd that breed prolifically throughout the waterways.

One bright winter's morning two friends cast their pike baits into a deep channel at the extreme end of the freshwater section just a few hundred yards from the more brackish water where there was a good chance of catching a flounder or a mullet. For the first hour the two big, bright pike floats bobbed about with not a sign of a fish. The two men lost interest as the icy wind gradually numbed them. They left their baits fishing and wandered off with their dogs at heel to try to warm up. Returning some ten minutes later they discovered that one rod had disappeared. At first they thought it might have been stolen, but that seemed unlikely in such a remote spot.

Then one of the fishermen spotted the missing pike float far away down the river. They gave chase, and having caught up with the float realised that somewhere down in the water beneath it was a pike that had hooked itself. But this was a wide river and there was no way to reach the float. Then,

20 yards (18.3m) upstream of the float, they saw the rod. There was only one thing to do. They shouted 'Fetch!' to the best of the two dogs and in an instant the big Labrador was powering through the water. When it reached the rod, the dog grabbed the cork handle and turned for the shore. It swam a few feet but was then unceremoniously tugged in the opposite direction. The pike was being played by the Labrador.

Now this was a dog that did not like to give up. It had swum much bigger, colder rivers than this and having been told to bring this curiously lively stick to its master it was intent on doing so, come what may. Thus began a 20-minute battle between a determined Labrador and an equally determined pike. At the end of that time the Labrador managed to reach the bank. Luckily it was a bank that shelved gradually away and the Labrador, having backed out of the water, kept hold of the rod and continued to back up until the pike came bouncing on to the shore. The fish – probably the only fish ever to be played and landed by a Labrador – weighed 11lb (5kg).

The one slightly unfortunate result of the whole affair was that the dog developed a taste for fishing. Whenever its owner hooked a fish from then on, the Labrador would bark and howl until the fish had been landed or until he had been given the rod so he could land the fish. On quiet, expensive fisheries the noise of the fish-mad dog became such an embarrassment that the fisherman often had to leave his faithful friend at home. But in the remaining six years of its life the fishing Labrador managed to land several more pike as well as a number of trout, two eels and a 3lb (1.4kg) chub.

MAGGOT BOX
ENGLAND, 1965

He was a little-known author, the last of that now vanished species of professional hack who, given a good brief and a reasonable amount of time, could turn out a decent workmanlike book on pretty much any subject. The freelance nature of his work also meant he had plenty of time to pursue his favourite sport – fishing. To be absolutely precise, he liked fishing the Thames and was often to be found wandering the riverbank in search of a forgotten backwater or a deep eddy that might contain a 5lb (2.3kg) chub or a 10lb (4.5kg) barbel or even, that most rare thing, a Thames trout.

On this particular day he was travelling to Windsor on the train from Paddington. Usually, he avoided the rush hour period and set off long before most travellers were even out of bed, but today he'd overslept and was now sitting in a crowded carriage surrounded by smartly dressed businessmen, mothers, children, students and tourists.

Our fisherman author didn't carry much with him in the way of tackle but he liked to take plenty of bait and on this occasion he had a truly massive baitbox filled to the very brim with some of the biggest, liveliest maggots he'd ever seen. The box must have contained at least two gallons of the little larvae.

The train was hot and crowded. The fisherman was tired. He soon fell fast asleep and suddenly, without knowing quite where he was, he was woken by deafening shouts and screams. At first he thought the train must have crashed. All along the carriage men, women and children were jumping about and uttering loud cries of disgust and fear. The fisherman was stunned – or at least he was until he happened to glance down at his tackle bag and baitbox. Somehow the baitbox had managed to tip over on its side and its lid had come off. Well over half the maggots had spilled on to the carriage floor. While he'd been asleep the motion of the train and the maggots' ceaseless crawling had distributed them evenly over virtually the whole of the carriage from one end to the other.

Thinking he was very likely to be lynched if found out, the intrepid angler hastily picked up his bits and pieces and made a quick getaway through the connecting door into the next carriage. Having carefully replaced the baitbox lid he settled down for a further nap.

TWO-LEGGED FISH

ENGLAND, 1965

It's a sad fact but a fact nonetheless that fishermen have to share rivers and lakes with other water users. The problem for fishermen is that they need quiet to get the best out of their pastime, while other water users often like to make as much noise and disturbance as possible. Water skiers are a curse, canoeists a damn nuisance and boating holidaymakers even worse.

Sometimes conflicts arise and boaters and anglers have even been known to come to blows. More amusingly, anglers fishing the stretch of the Thames that runs through Oxford have at times taken their revenge on the arrogance of passing college boats by accidentally catapulting large quantities of maggots at the occupants.

However, problems like these are thankfully rare on the upper reaches of the Thames, and Buscot, with its moss-covered weir and air of Victorian innocence, was a quiet backwater with few boats in the 1960s. Fishermen in pursuit of the massive barbel that skulked beneath the foaming waters of the weir had it all to themselves, which is why the legend of what the locals jokingly called the biggest talking fish ever landed in Britain became part of fishing folklore.

It all started on a sunny day in August. A London club had come up to fish the stretch of water below – but also including – the weir and they were not having an easy time of it. Water levels were low, the river was sluggish and the fish were not in a taking mood.

But the 50-odd fishermen pegged out at 30-yard (27.4m) intervals along the banks stayed put. One or two gave up and enjoyed the view; some found a book or a newspaper somewhere in their capacious bags and began to read; others discreetly reeled in their lines, stretched themselves out on the warm earth and fell asleep. One fisherman, pegged about halfway along the mile (1.6km) of river devoted to the match, was determined to catch something. He'd done badly in the last two matches and was keen to at least avoid a blank despite the fact that, on this hot and unforgiving August day, most of the club was likely to remain fishless.

A small group of what this particular fisherman assumed were picnickers had settled on the far bank about 400 yards (366m) downstream. The fisherman noted their arrival and then forgot all about them. As the afternoon grew hotter, more fishermen gave up the unequal struggle and settled down for a snooze. Three who had long ago surrendered decided to wander along the bank and see if anyone had caught anything. They arrived at the peg where our determined fisherman continued to try as hard as he could just in time to see him strike and apparently make contact with a good fish. They were astonished and said so. The man in contact with the fish was so excited and simultaneously terrified that this monster chub or barbel would get off that he spoke not a word. But inwardly he was exultant, knowing that if he could get this fish safely to the bank he would win the match by a wide margin.

His rod was bent double, line occasionally slipped from the reel as the fish moved downstream, but it was a solid, seemingly immovable weight. The fisherman put as much pressure on it as he dared and the minutes slipped by. This was unprecedented. He could see his line entering the water about 50 yards (45.7m) downstream, but it was moving in circles. Then it edged slowly towards the opposite bank before returning, quiet and unhurried, to the centre of the river. Still the full pressure of the rod was having absolutely no effect.

The fisherman was beginning to despair. Behind him and around him a small crowd of his clubmates had gathered as word of the epic battle spread along the river. And they were all watching when the fisherman suddenly seemed to be getting somewhere. This monster of the deep was no longer 50 yards (45.7m) away. It was virtually opposite the angler, right in the middle of the river.

Then with a great boil it came to the surface. It was a diver, fully kitted out with rubber wetsuit and oxygen tank. With rod still bent double and his line clearly running down to a point on the diver's left leg, the fisherman could only stand and stare. He was speechless. The diver – one of that small group of apparent picnickers downstream on the far bank – was unfortunately not in the least lost for words. He took off his facemask and hurled abuse at the poor fisherman for a full two minutes. The gist of it seemed to be that a very expensive diving suit now had a nasty little leak in it caused by a size-14 hook and a ball of cheese paste.

That August match went down in the club's history books as the worst in terms of fishing but by far the best for entertainment.

FALSE ALARM

WALES, 1966

Four fishing friends decided to spend a weekend fishing a famous Welsh lake. They had never before fished for Arctic char, that unique survival of the last Ice Age that still exists in small numbers in certain English and Welsh waters. The friends had read the few books that exist about this strange fish, and had the right tackle. They were determined not to be side-tracked by the far more numerous trout in the lake.

The hotel where the four friends stayed was one of those big old Edwardian affairs with endless corridors and hidden staircases for the servants. As luck would have it, the hotel owner was unable to give them a room each so they had to share: two were put in a large room on the first floor and two had a smaller room on the second floor, but none of this mattered since they would be out on the lake from dawn till dusk.

Their first day on the lake passed uneventfully. For hours they drifted across the water – which was nearly 1 mile (1.6km) in length – towing their deeply sunk teams of flies. As dusk began to fall they realised they had been fishing for 14 hours without even seeing a fish of any species, let alone hooking a real char.

It was probably this long fruitless wait that led to what followed back at the hotel because, frankly, the four friends were rather bored and, their efforts having proved fruitless, they – or at least two of them – were determined to have some fun. After dinner the two friends whose room was on the first floor hatched a plot to give their friends on the second floor the fright of their lives in the middle of the night. The plan was simply to wait until their friends were asleep and then rush in, throwing water everywhere and shouting that the hotel was on fire.

Consequently, the two friends, still the worse for wear after several bottles of wine at dinner, burst into the second-floor room where their friends were asleep. They switched on all the lights and threw their two buckets of water at the bed shouting, 'Fire! Fire!' at the top of their voices and it was only after the waters had settled all over the bedcovers, the floor and a nearby desk that the practical jokers noticed that sitting up in bed were not their two friends, but an elderly man and his wife, both looking extremely wet and extremely angry.

The original inhabitants of the room – the two fishermen – had that very morning agreed to swap with the Bishop of Bath and Wells and his wife who were holidaying in the region.

The young men were so embarrassed that, without saying a word, they ran from the room, packed their bags, leapt in their car and drove off, resolving to phone the friends they'd left behind and explain their terrible mistake and hasty departure.

In the morning the two friends still in the hotel got wind of the night's extraordinary events, but having come a long way they decided they might as well continue fishing. Within half an hour of setting off across the lake they'd hooked and landed two Arctic char, each weighing a little over 1lb (0.45kg). To this day one of those fish is still kept in the Natural History Museum in London.

GIANT TIDDLER

ENGLAND, 1966

It was the worst match the club members could remember. Thirty-five fishermen strung out along one of the best bits of the Thames and three hours into the five-hour match not a single sizeable fish had been landed.

Today when match fishermen can weigh in any fish they catch, however small, it probably seems strange that there was a time right up into the 1970s when, in the Thames catchment area, each individual fish species had a minimum size it had to reach before it could be weighed in a match. This made the competition far more interesting, but often left one feeling sorry for the fish that were frequently seen being stretched along rulers in the hope that they might just make the requisite length. When the length requirement vanished so too did matches that produced a situation at the end of the day where there were simply no sizeable fish to weigh in.

But on this day in 1966 a howling gale was blowing, ice formed continually on the fishermen's rod rings, and hands were completely numbed despite thick gloves and mittens. Quite a few fish were caught despite the appalling conditions but they were all far too small to weigh in.

The weather worsened as the afternoon wore on. Still the fishermen battled on, for there was a big cash prize and everyone knew that one good fish would probably be enough to win. With five minutes to go before the end of the match word had spread up and down the river that not one 'go-er', not one sizeable fish of any species, had been caught. Groups of fishermen stood around glumly or tried cracking jokes while making desperate efforts to keep warm.

When the final whistle went, club officials set up the scales and waited to see if by some miracle someone from the far end of the venue – almost 1 mile (1.6km) away – had managed to land a fish. Twenty minutes passed and the men gathered around the scales – including the majority of the 35 who had been fishing – decided that enough was enough. Only one or two anglers had not yet turned up and it was time to pack away the scales, get back on the coach and turn all the heaters on.

Then, just in the instant that the decision had been made, a ten-year-old boy who was fishing his very first match came up carrying his canvas bucket filled with water. The older men, who between them probably had centuries of experience, couldn't believe it. What on earth did he have in there?

The boy reached the scales and said proudly. 'I caught a gudgeon.'

'Let's have a look at it then,' came the reply.

Gingerly the boy tipped the water out of his bucket and a bright, bouncing gudgeon dropped into the weigh basket. The club official lifted the fish out of the basket and measured it. Not a breath came from the 30 anglers gathered in a tight circle. The gudgeon measured fractionally over the required 5½in (14cm). It was a 'go-er'.

The boy beamed at the men, who looked decidedly sheepish. Back in the weigh basket the gudgeon tipped the scales at 15 drams, a fraction under 1oz (28g). There was a huge cheer when the announcement was made that the young lad on his first outing had beaten the club's most experienced fishermen and he was carried shoulder high to the coach with a £20 note – the prize for the day – firmly lodged in his trouser pocket.

HOOKS GALORE

ENGLAND, 1967

Many people who don't fish think fishing a most bizarre pastime. 'I wouldn't have the patience to sit there all day waiting for something to happen,' is the non-angler's common response to the suggestion that he or she might like a day on the river. But if keen fishermen – and women – might dispute the dullness of their sport, they would more readily accept that some very bizarre things are prone to happen when one is fishing. Every coarse, sea and game fisher has a tale or two of oddity and coincidence, but few are stranger than the tale of the lost and regained Isle of Wight carp.

At the end of a long-disused track just a few miles from the town of Newport there was an old flooded gravel working called Dodnor Pond. The pond was run by an elderly couple who lived in a tumbledown cottage right at the edge of the water. They sold day tickets to fish the lake which, despite having been a scene of industry 30 years earlier, was now a very pretty, wildlife-rich place. The fishing, which seemed to be known only to local schoolboys, was absolutely wonderful. All the carp in the lake were wild commons in beautiful condition and their average weight was about 5lb (2.3kg), which may not sound much but these carp were super-fit and sleek. When a carp was hooked it would shoot off across the lake at an unbelievable speed. For that first unstoppable run the only tactic, however strong one's tackle, was to let the fish go. Because the lake was fairly shallow right across its four acres the carp would often leap and somersault like salmon. It was a truly magical place.

The lake had countless reed-fringed bays and corners overhung with willow. It also had the great advantage, from a fisherman's point of view, of being ideal for fishing floating crust, easily the most exciting way to catch carp. The trick was to push your hook through a piece of crust the size of a matchbox, dunk it in the water just once to give it some weight and then cast it out to the edge of the nearest reed bed. You then had to keep absolutely motionless and await events. More carp were always caught by those able to keep really very still indeed. Fishermen addicted to moving about and adjusting their tackle or talking to their neighbours almost never caught a thing.

On this particular day a schoolboy from London had just landed a wonderful 7-pounder (3.2kg). Having weighed his fish and recorded the details in the fishery logbook he put it gently back in the water, but not before removing at least seven half-rusted old hooks stuck in the poor animal's bottom lip. They had clearly been there for some time, but other than making the fish look like a punk rocker with too many piercings, the hooks were quite obviously doing the fish no harm at all. It was as fat as butter and fighting fit.

The young man extricated all the hooks but one, a big vicious-looking brass hook with a fearsome barb. Getting that barb out would probably have done more harm than good, but at least he'd removed the others.

The fish went back and the schoolboy wandered off to eat his packed lunch. An hour later he was back in his favourite position. He tried an extra-large piece of crust and flicked it out to the very point of a narrow peninsula of reeds that jutted out well into the middle of the lake. After watching the crust for what seemed like an eternity, the schoolboy noticed that it was beginning to sink. Normally he would have reeled in and put on a fresh piece of bread, but for now he was happy to see what would happen if he simply left his bait on the bottom. Hardly had it vanished from sight than the line began to shoot away across the lake. The schoolboy lifted his rod and slammed into a fish that immediately rocketed up from the depths and soared across the surface of the lake.

The super-fit fish took ten minutes to subdue, but when it reached the net the schoolboy fisherman got the shock of his life. He lifted the carp out of the net and saw that his hook had passed through the eye of an old hook left in the carp's bottom lip. If that wasn't unusual enough, he also saw that the old hook was brass with a fearsome barb on it. This was the very same fish he'd hooked and landed earlier that same day.

BOSUN'S ANTICS

ENGLAND, 1968

The Avon below Salisbury was a wonderful mixed fishery until abstraction and pollution reduced water levels and water quality. Now the great shoals of sleek grayling and butter-coloured trout are largely gone, although coarse fish remain in reduced numbers. Somehow, despite reassuring noises from the scientists about water quality, the river no longer sparkles.

But back in the 1960s the fishing could be fabulous and an occasional salmon was even taken. An elderly fisherman who came down every Wednesday to fish the London Anglers Association water always arrived with his old black Labrador. The old man was unusual in that he was a keen coarse fisherman who, when he thought conditions were right, fished the fly. He put his coarse fish back as gently as possible, but any trout unlucky enough to be seduced by his fly was taken home for supper.

Other fishermen noticed that when the old man hooked a fish his dog became wildly excited, jumping and almost turning somersaults until the fish was in the net. One day another regular got chatting to the old man and commented on the antics of his dog. 'Oh, he thinks I'm going to send him to get the fish,' said the old man. 'I used to fish on a very difficult water where you'd hook a fish and it'd tear off into a thick weed bed from which it could only rarely be extracted. When Bosun here was a puppy I gradually taught him to paddle out to this weed bed and either swim down and grab the fish while it was still on the hook or, if he couldn't do that, at least try to move the fish out of the weeds. Nine times out of ten it worked wonderfully well and I caught a lot more fish that I would have otherwise. But then we moved and I no longer fished that river. I got a ticket for this water and, so far, I've never had to call on Bosun's services. As you can see he gets pretty cross about it!' The young man listened to the old fellow talking and assumed he was being teased so he nodded, said good morning and walked off to fish a distant meadow.

'I think he's lost his marbles,' he mumbled to himself and thought nothing more of it. Two weeks later he happened to be crossing one of the carriers – the man-made streams that criss-cross the old water meadows below Salisbury – when he spotted the old man again. From the look of his rod the old man had hooked a good fish and since it was quite clearly a fly rod it must be a big trout or a small salmon.

The younger man thought the least he could do was wander along and offer to net the fish, and he was halfway across the intervening meadow when he noticed the dog running away from the old man. Then in an instant he saw the dog turn – almost as a bowler turns towards the wicket before beginning his run – and dash towards the water. The dog flew into the air and landed in the carrier about halfway across with a huge splash. The dog glanced about him continually as he swam across; then as he neared a thick, overhanging willow he ducked under the water and vanished from sight. Minutes seemed to pass and then the dog reappeared with a trout in its mouth – and a very fine trout it was too.

The dog arrived on the bank and presented the trout to its master as if it were a pheasant. When the younger man finally came up to the old man the fish – which looked as if it weighed about 2lb (0.9kg) – had been unhooked and stowed away in the old man's knapsack.

'I must admit I didn't believe a word of it when you told me about your dog,' said the young man.

'Quite all right,' came the reply, 'it does sound like a bit of a tall story, but Bosun has landed hundreds of fish like that. I'm only sad he doesn't get the chance more often. That's why he jumps around so much – it's as if he's asking me to go and fish somewhere I'm more likely to get snagged up!'

And with that he whistled up the dog and wandered away.

TANK MANOEUVRES

LONDON, 1968

Where the Grand Union Canal in West London runs past Kensal Cemetery the roach and bream fishing is, or at least was, excellent. In the 1960s and early 1970s huge bags of fish were taken by those in the know, along with big individual specimens. Bream to 7lb (3.2kg) were common and roach over the magical 2lb (0.9kg) mark were seen regularly.

On a bright sunny summer day in 1968 one angler using hemp as bait caught three 2lb roach in three consecutive casts – an astonishing achievement from a fishery littered with supermarket trolleys and rubbish of all kinds.

On the towpath side of the canal opposite the cemetery there was a long abandoned gasworks, which retained the old basins or docks where the barges bringing coal had once unloaded their cargoes and then turned, before heading back off up the narrow canal.

To get into the basins the narrowboats had first to turn off the main canal and go under steeply arched towpath bridges and it was here that the biggest bags were taken.

Among canal enthusiasts these were golden days on a golden water, but there were always complaints that the canal did not offer a greater variety of sport – old-timers remembered the days when astonishingly the canal had contained large perch and pike and even a few huge carp. Where had they all gone? No one knew.

When work finally began on the old gasworks and some

of the equipment was taken down and dismantled, a most extraordinary thing was discovered.

One of the water towers that was a good 100 yards (91.4m) from the canal and propped up 20ft (6.1m) above the ground on steel legs was found to contain numerous giant perch. Local fishermen were astonished – how on earth had these specimen fish got into the water towers? There were no inlet or outlet pipes to the canal so the whole thing was a mystery.

At last a biologist came up with a plausible explanation: ducks and other birds that came to the water tower occasionally had probably carried fish eggs on their legs from other waters and the eggs had then hatched in the tower tank. But what they fed on while they grew defeated even the biologists. Flies landing on the water would hardly keep a healthy population of perhaps 30 or 40 perch and allow them to grow into 1- and 2-pounders (0.45–0.9kg), but that's how many were found.

Now the old power station is long gone and expensive – if rather ugly – flats line the canal at Kensal Rise but the descendants of those big perch may still be in the canal ready for a skilful patient angler, for when the tank was emptied the fish were all released into the canal itself.

WRITING IT ALL DOWN
ENGLAND, 1969

The Knightsbridge corner of the Serpentine Lake in London's Hyde Park offered urban youngsters the chance to fish for free until relatively recently. All that was necessary to fish this lake and a dozen others in different London parks, was a letter to the Parks' Superintendent requesting permission, so every year the letters flowed in from schoolchildren across the capital. One or two adults had always requested permits too and among these was one extraordinary man. He was probably in his sixties, very tall and very thin, and he fished using the longest rod anyone had ever seen. He didn't bother with the other parks – Hyde Park and the Knightsbridge corner were enough for him. But he fished only one day a week. Always a Saturday and always from the same park bench. He had never missed a Saturday in any season dating back longer than anyone could remember.

But it wasn't just these regular habits that made this particular fisherman so unusual. At a time when continental-style pole fishing was virtually unheard of in England he used an old-fashioned hollow-cane roach pole – a piece of equipment much loved by elderly cockneys – of enormous length. Now the thing about roach poles is that they are very long because you don't use a reel with them. Just a tough piece of elastic tied to the tip (and designed to prevent a break caused by a bigger fish) and then your nylon. But our tall, thin fisherman had fitted his roach pole with rings and a big old-fashioned centre-pin reel. The reel was an Alcock Aerial, one of the most highly prized of collectors' reels, but very much an antique.

Youngsters who were new to the Knightsbridge corner would secretly laugh at the thin man with the roach pole, but only until one of the more experienced boys pointed out that the thin man might look odd, but he was singularly good at fishing. In fact, for the boys who fished the Knightsbridge corner regularly the thin man was something of a hero. While they might catch a few fish, perhaps a dozen on a good day, the tall, thin fisherman might easily catch 40 or 50 and his were almost always on average bigger than anyone else's.

His technique, like everything else about him, was eccentric. He never used maggots, which were almost universal among the other anglers. He never hurried and he never showed the least signs of excitement when he hooked and landed a specimen that had every other angler gazing at him open-mouthed.

While the boys were delighted if they caught roach and rudd, the thin man always seemed able to find the bright gold – and much coveted – crucian carp. On one memorable day he caught a dozen beauties all over 2lb (4.5kg) before topping that remarkable success with the only catfish anyone had ever seen caught. The thin man's technique and attitude seemed to rub off on the boys, who concentrated harder when he was around and tried to emulate his calm, measured approach. They also noted how carefully he unhooked his fish and how gently he returned them.

But perhaps the most astonishing thing of all about the tall, thin fisherman was that for the 30 years he had fished the Knightsbridge corner of the Serpentine he had noted down the length and weight of every single fish – however tiny and apparently insignificant – in a series of notebooks. Each book was lined and leather-bound. Each page had a heading giving the date and some brief note about the weather. Then below that came a single line for each fish. He was on his sixtieth notebook and judging by his tiny, neat handwriting those 60 fat books must have contained the details of thousands of long-dead fish.

Why the thin fisherman did all this no one knew. Some said he was a disappointed Oxford academic who had turned to fishing as a relief from the insanities of university life. Others said he was probably a spy. Whatever or whoever he was, on the first day of the season one year he didn't turn up and he was never heard of or seen again.

BLEAK OUTLOOK
ENGLAND, 1972

During the 1970s bleak numbers in the River Thames reached extraordinary levels. The bleak is a small, silver fish not unlike a sprat, and although it is a splendid-looking little fellow it has one major disadvantage from the angler's point of view: it rarely weighs more than 1oz (28g).

From Richmond to Windsor it was difficult to put a bait in the water without immediately suffering the attentions of hordes of these little fish, which was enormously frustrating for anglers seeking bigger quarry. The problem was exacerbated by the fact that maggots have always been the most popular bait on the lower Thames and bleak love maggots. Some fishermen got round the problem by using other baits, but the match-fishing fraternity decided they might as well make a virtue of necessity and fish for 'bloody nuisances' as the bleak were known.

Some huge bags of bleak were taken with one of the most notable falling to a Frenchman fishing 1 mile (1.6km) or so above Richmond Bridge. In a five-hour match he landed almost a thousand bleak – that's an average of more than three fish landed per minute. No one knows if he stopped for lunch – if he did he would have had to increase that average significantly just to catch up!

HAIR OF THE DOG

SCOTLAND, 1972

A famous gillie who'd worked on the Spey for decades used regularly to catch fish when others found it extremely difficult or impossible. Some put it down to his enormous experience while others thought it was just that the gillie knew the water so well he could time his fishing to perfection.

One day he'd done particularly well whenever his guest handed him the rod and went off for a while. Each time the fisherman returned he found that the gillie had landed another fish. After three fish had been caught in this way the fisherman decided to stick it out. He fished hard for a couple of hours. Nothing. It was puzzling because the fisherman was experienced and extremely knowledgeable. Eventually he stopped fishing, offered the gillie a dram from his flask and asked him how he did it.

Feeling sorry for the fisherman who was an old friend, the gillie looked about quickly and then beckoned him to come closer.

'Dog hair,' said the gillie.

'What?' said the guest.

'Dog hair,' came the reply.

'What on earth has dog hair got to do with it?'

Each time you went away I tied a bit of my old Alsatian's fur to the hook. On a dour day like this it can make all the difference.

The fisherman clearly didn't believe a word of it so the gillie took the rod, reeled in and, having fished around in his pocket, tied on a short tuft of blackish hair. Five minutes later he was into a good fish. The fisherman was astonished. This time instead of removing the dog hair when he handed the rod back to the fisherman the gillie left it on and within minutes another salmon lay on the bank.

The gillie insisted the trick did not always work, but when everything else had been tried it was, he said, always worth a shot.

ON THE RUN

ENGLAND, 1973

The riverkeeper on a famous beat of a very famous English trout river dined out for many years on the strange tale of the day he caught two schoolboy poachers red-handed.

It was during what was generally considered the very best period of the spring. Trout had been rising freely throughout the previous week and some fine fish had been landed by visitors and local anglers. But locals and visitors had one thing in common: they were paying a great deal of money for the privilege of fishing. The morning came when the riverkeeper did his usual rounds and, coming along the bank towards the best pool, he spotted two schoolboys. They were undoubtedly poachers, but how on earth was he to catch them? He could just chase them off, but local schoolboys had been a particular nuisance of late and he was determined to make an example of this pair.

The riverkeeper took a big detour around the field on the edge of which the boys were fishing. He then crept along the far side of a hedge that would eventually bring him – still concealed – to within 60ft (18.3m) of the boys. As he made his way along he noticed at least one thing in the boys' favour – they were not using worms as most of the village boys did. They were at least fly fishing, but at their feet was a large, ominous-looking canvas bag. The riverkeeper felt sure that the bag was filled with his beautiful brown trout.

The riverkeeper waited just where the hawthorn hedge

reached the riverbank. Then, having got his breath back and waited until the boys looked particularly relaxed and unsuspecting, he jumped through the hedge and ran as fast as he could towards them. One boy stood stock still while the other made a run for it. Ignoring the first boy, the riverkeeper set off in pursuit of the runner. Two fields further along he caught up with him.

'How dare you poach my river,' said the riverkeeper. 'You boys think you can do what you like, but I've had enough. I'm taking you to the police and they can tell your parents.'

The riverkeeper grabbed the boy's collar and began to lead him along the bank.

'But I've got a licence to fish,' said the boy.

'Don't be ridiculous,' came the reply.

'But I have – look!' said the young man. And sure enough his papers were all in order and he was perfectly entitled to fish. The riverkeeper was astonished.

'Why on earth did you run away if you had a licence?' he asked.

'Well, I had a licence, but my friend didn't!' The riverkeeper laughed so much at how he'd been duped that he patted the schoolboy on his back and sent him on his way.

STABBED

AUSTRALIA, 1976

The black marlin swordfish is a fearsome adversary, but also one of the most sporting fish in the world. An average swordfish may weigh 300–400lb (136–181kg) and they fight like the devil. Fishermen have been yanked overboard after hooking one of these spectacular fish, but a certain swordfish hunter experienced a far more dangerous incident one summer off the coast of Australia.

He hooked his swordfish just after lunch and four hours later it was still taking line and jumping spectacularly high into the air some 300 yards (274m) behind the boat. The fisherman had to fight for every 12in (30.5cm) of line and as he sat strapped into the specially made fighting chair his face poured with sweat in his struggle to keep control of a swordfish estimated at 400lb (181kg). Each time he doggedly gained a few feet of line, the swordfish stripped off several dozen yards with what seemed like the greatest of ease. But at last the fish neared the boat and the fisherman asked to be released from the fighting chair to ease his aching muscles. The fish was clearly beaten and any further runs were likely to be minor affairs and easily controlled. The swordfish was drawn alongside the boat and the skipper readied the gaff. By this time the fisherman was standing almost beside the skipper and leaning a little out of the gunwales where the fish lay on the surface of the water. A second later the apparently docile fish lashed its great tail and the movement pushed it almost vertically out of the water and up the side of the boat. As it rose the fish's great spear-like bill hit the fisherman in the top part of his chest near the shoulder. In the panic of the sudden movement, which was followed by the fish being successfully gaffed and brought aboard, no one was aware of the wound in the fisherman's chest. The fisherman himself hardly noticed in the excitement of landing such a good fish. It was only when a semblance of calm returned to the boat that the fisherman looked down and realised that the marlin's spike had passed right through his chest and out of his back. By now his shirt, both back and front, was completely soaked in blood. Seconds later the fisherman collapsed, suffering from blood loss. It was only the quick thinking of the skipper that saved his life. The wound was packed with rags torn from an old shirt and the boat raced for the home port nearly an hour away. It was touch and go, but they got the fisherman to hospital – just in time. He was kept on massive doses of antibiotics for several weeks and was told that he was very lucky indeed to be alive.

But like most anglers the injured man could not keep away from his favourite sport for long. Within a few months he was back out at sea in search of an even bigger swordfish.

OTTER SPOTTER

ENGLAND, 1979

The River Tyne was once a very good salmon and sea trout river but heavy industry began to destroy the river in the nineteenth century. By the 1970s the few salmon that were still getting up the river could do so only on the highest of flood tides when these were combined with heavy rainfall to bring the freshwater level of the river up. In these circumstances the sheer quantity of water meant that the fish could rush through the normally filthy lower reaches to the cleaner water beyond. By the time they reached Wylam, perhaps 20 miles (32.2km) inland, the River Tyne was pretty much as it had always been – clean and free of obstructions. And it was at Wylam that a young man from Newcastle University enjoyed an extraordinary wildlife encounter.

One of the best things about fishing is that it keeps the fisher in much closer touch with nature than almost any other pastime. For most anglers an hour or two on the riverbank is just not enough – it's got to be the whole day and a whole day during which one keeps, generally speaking, as quiet as possible.

Our young man from the university was keeping very quiet one summer morning because the river seemed to be bursting with fish. Trout and salmon appeared to be jumping everywhere and he already had two good trout in the bag. When the tide began to come in – the Tyne even 20 miles inland is still tidal – the fishing got even better, but the young man had to switch to coarse tackle as the fly was suddenly much less effective.

He was happily casting and re-casting when, just a few feet from the tip of his rod, an otter's head suddenly popped into view. Now there have always been otters in the Tyne, but here was a fine, big one just a few miles from the busiest and dirtiest city in the North East. The fisherman froze. He let his float swing round in the current until it tangled in the bankside vegetation, but he didn't care. Suddenly fishing had taken a back seat to the marvellous spectacle of this wonderful creature staring straight at him from just a few feet away.

Then as quickly as it had appeared the otter vanished in a swirl. The fisherman still did nothing. He kept absolutely still and waited, all the time hoping for another sight of this splendid animal. Just as he was about to give up and resume his fishing, the sleek otter appeared again, this time out towards the middle of the river. Man and otter stared at each other for some moments. Then, hardly believing that this could be happening, the young man spotted two more otters just 10ft (3m) from the first. Perhaps the young man was particularly good at keeping absolutely still or perhaps these were unusual otters, but whatever the explanation these most elusive and shy creatures began to play in the river right in front of him. It was as if he wasn't there or as if the otters knew that he would not interrupt them. The young man witnessed the kind of intimate otter behaviour it normally takes trained naturalists and film-makers months if not years to observe.

The otters continued to dive and splash each other for the next 20 minutes and then suddenly it was over. But still the young man waited, keeping absolutely motionless. Maybe they would reappear. Nothing. Eventually the fisherman realised that they would not return and with a heavy heart he retrieved his line, untangled his float and began to fish again. First cast he hooked what felt like a decent fish and he began to play it towards the waiting net. Then something odd happened. There was an almighty tug on the line as if a 20lb (9.1kg) salmon had attached itself to the line. In the next instant the line fell slack. He reeled in and discovered the front half only of a trout that would have weighed perhaps ¾lb (0.3kg), which is pretty good for the Tyne. The back end of the fish had been bitten clean off – by an otter. Nothing else could have done such damage and it explained the heavy tug on the line. It was as if the otters were saying, 'How dare you fish here – this is our bit of water!'

WEIGHTS AND MEASURES

ENGLAND, 1979

Most fishermen trust each other. If your fishing friends say they have caught or lost such and such a fish you believe them, notwithstanding the old adage about fisherman exaggerating the size of the one that got away. The truth is that there is no point lying about an unusual fish or a huge specimen because the fact that you yourself know you haven't caught it is enough to ruin any pleasure you might gain from the astonished looks on the faces of your fellow anglers. Of course there are always exceptions to this rule.

One angler regularly broke all the rules and surprised his friends with a series of astonishing successes. It took years to catch him out. Whenever he caught a fish it always weighed a great deal more than any similar fish caught by anyone else. If it was a roach it was always over the magic 2lb (0.9kg) mark; if it was tench it was always a superb 6- or even 7-pounder (2.7–3.2kg). If it was a pike it never weighed less than 20lb (9.1kg). It seemed that this particular fisherman could do no wrong. Like most of his friends the fisherman used his own set of scales – they were of the highest quality and a very good make – and because his friends thought he would never lie to them it was simply assumed that he was a brilliant and lucky angler.

After a year in which he managed to land no fewer than 17 pike over 20lb (9.1kg), not to mention numerous other specimens, he was given his fishing club's highest award at the annual dinner. Two days later the fisherman's best friend and neighbour became a father. The friend was also a keen fisherman and he decided on this particular morning that he would weigh his new son. Try as he might he could not find his scales so he popped round to his friend's to borrow a set. It was then that the explanation for all those heavy pike, perch, roach and tench became apparent for, according to his friend's scales, the two-day-old baby weighed 22lb (10kg)!

RECORD BAG

ENGLAND, 1981

Fly fishing for trout, particularly brown trout, is not easy. In fact the whole point of fly fishing is that it should be difficult, for the poor old trout is a bit of a dimwit in the sense that he is far too easy to catch on bait or spinner. Fly fishing was introduced at least partly to protect the trout itself from wholesale slaughter for there is no doubt that uncontrolled use of worms or maggots as bait would leave most trout fisheries entirely devoid of fish. Of course fly fishing is a highly satisfying way of catching your trout, particularly if you are of that school of fly fisherman who likes to try to use a fly that imitates exactly the real fly that the trout are taking at any particular time.

However, one young man, fishing a North Country river, found that the legendary difficulties of fly fishing for trout had been wildly exaggerated. His fly seemed to be favoured as if it had all the irresistible qualities of a large, juicy lobworm.

The young man actually had very little experience of fly fishing. He was a coarse fisherman with enormous experience of catching chub, dace and barbel but, having moved to the north of England where most river fishing meant trout or salmon, he thought he would try his hand at this supposedly challenging art. He bought all the latest – and most expensive – equipment, read every book he could lay his hands on and bought a ticket for the nearest stretch of his local river. Though once a very fine salmon fishing river, the local water had suffered terribly from heavy industrial pollution and only a few hardy salmon still ran the gauntlet up to the spawning redds. But the lack of salmon had at least reduced the cost of the fishing.

On his first visit to the river, armed with his new tackle, the fisherman felt a little unsure of himself. All the books he'd read suggested fly fishing was a complicated business with an almost infinite number of possible variables – choice of fly could depend on temperature, light levels, water flow, time of year or any combination of these factors. How on earth was he to manage? He decided he would give it a try and if he failed he would return to his beloved coarse fishing.

He reached the first pool, selected a small black fly (one of his books had advised – 'If in doubt, start with a small black fly'), and started to fish. His initial cast was, as he himself later admitted, completely hopeless: the line fell in a heap and the fly landed barely 15ft (4.6m) from the bank. But no sooner had it landed than a huge boil seemed to engulf it. The fisherman was so astonished he forgot to strike and by the time he did pick up his rod the trout – if that is what it was – had long since departed.

He checked his little black fly, which seemed to be fine, and made another attempt at casting. But he was shaking so much at what had just happened – after all it could have been a salmon – that he messed the whole thing up and, once again, his line and fly dropped in a messy pile on the water.

'Nothing could possibly take that fly!' he mused. But he decided to let the current pull his line straight before trying once again to get this casting business right. The fly came round in the current and he began to reel in a little before embarking on the next cast. Now, all the books he'd read said that a trout takes only when a fly that looks like an insect starts moving through the water in a natural manner.

On this occasion the young man's fly must have appeared to be swimming strongly against the current as it was reeled in; despite that huge apparent disadvantage the next thing that happened was a pull that tore the line out of the young man's hand. Next minute he was playing a very good fish. It turned out to be a trout weighing a little over 2lb (0.9kg). It was a lovely fish. Fit-looking, beautifully coloured and with a full tail. It looked like a wild trout rather than a fat old stocked fish with half its fins missing.

The fisherman was so delighted that, inwardly, he swore he would be happy if that was his only fish of the day. But the very next cast – which improved a little in the wake of this unwarranted success – the young man hooked another trout that was, in size and appearance, identical to the first.

Soon trout number two was on the bank. For the next couple of hours every cast produced a take. Sometimes the young man mistimed his strike, on other occasions he hooked the fish only to lose it a few moments later. Most of the fish he landed were 2–3lb (0.9–1.4kg), but to his utter astonishment they just kept coming. Fish after fish – it was as though every square foot of river as far up and downstream as he could see was simply filled with fish. It didn't matter where he cast his fly. It didn't matter how badly he cast it. As soon as it hit the water it was taken. At one stage he looked at his fly and discovered it was so chewed that to all intents and purposes he was fishing with a bare hook with a black smudge on it.

By late afternoon he had caught more than 60 fish, and appalled by the slaughter he began to put them back. His back and arms ached from playing the fish. When he finally packed up he had to run to a phone and get his wife to bring a car to take the fish home. When he left he knew that he could have carried on catching fish well into the evening, but the truth was that he was almost sick of it. Trout fishing seemed far too simple, but despite the fact that this was the first time he'd ever tried it he knew that something was wrong. Something odd and inexplicable had happened to make this the most extraordinary day's fishing.

At home he telephoned his neighbours and filled their fridges with trout. Two days later he found out why he'd caught so many fish. He was reading the local paper when he came across a short item about a fish farm that had inadvertently left a large filter pipe open. The filter pipe led into the river and the fish farm had lost several thousand mature brown trout.

The fisherman decided that he would keep quiet about his day's trout fishing. He also decided that trout fishing was a mug's game – too easy, too artificial and too dispiriting. Next time he went fishing he would take his roach fishing gear.

THIN-LIPPED MULLET

ENGLAND, 1982

Christchurch Harbour in Dorset is one of the very few places in Britain where the angler has a chance of catching that most rare fish, the thin-lipped mullet. To the man on the Clapham omnibus the thin-lipped mullet looks exactly like the far more common thick-lipped variety, but the scientists tell us that the two are separate species. The difference – bizarrely, given the two names – has nothing to do with the size of the lips and, in fact, the only way to tell which is which is to examine the scales.

Be that as it may, it happens that Christchurch Harbour is home to a local population of thin-lipped mullet. If you catch a mullet in the harbour the chances are that it will be thin-lipped.

In 1982 sea fishermen used regularly to fish for the Christchurch thin-lips. There were plenty of them, they took spinners freely and they were hard fighters. Fishing for them from a small boat had another benefit: the British record for a thin-lipped mullet caught from a boat at that time stood at less than 2lb (0.9kg). The shore-caught record was much bigger and thick-lipped mullet in Christchurch Harbour were known to average just under the existing record. If ever a British record was just waiting to fall this was it.

Then one day it happened. A journalist from a fishing paper was out boat fishing in the harbour when, first cast, he hooked a mullet that weighed just over 2½lb (1.1kg). If it was confirmed to be a thin-lip this was the new British record. The journalist took his mullet to the fishery expert at London's Natural History Museum and sure enough the museum confirmed its thin-lipped status. The journalist went into the record books and the mullet went into the museum's stores, where it remains to this day alongside numerous fishery specimens collected by Darwin during the voyage of the *Beagle*. Until that thin-lipped mullet turned up for identification even the Natural History Museum's officials had never seen an example of the species.

The news of the latest British record took the angling world by storm. But inevitably, given the involvement of journalists, the story came out all wrong and even the *Angling Times,* once the authoritative voice of fishing, described the fish in a ground-breaking feature as a 'thin-legged mullet'.

But the record did not survive for long. After an epic battle in Christchurch Harbour the following year, an even bigger thin-lipped mullet was landed. This time the lucky angler was aged four.

CASTING PRACTICE

ENGLAND, 1983

Until the mid-1980s a small, family-owned firm of publishers still existed in Windsor. It was one of the last of those cranky firms that were soon to be bought up and ruined by massive publishing conglomerates more interested in management theories than producing things people might want to read.

Here in an old house the family firm had long published an angling magazine. It was the sort of magazine that assumed fishermen were able to read and were interested in things beyond the best float to use or the latest space-age rod-making material. The magazine's editor remembered a time when fishermen were literate and well read and he produced the sort of magazine his readers wanted to read. One of the perks of working on a fishing magazine in those days was the chance to test and review new items of fishing tackle, which is why astonished passers-by occasionally saw nets left hanging to dry from the windows or glimpsed what looked uncannily like a salmon fisherman casting from a first-floor balcony.

On one occasion the reviews editor was presented with a box of newly minted American lures. Like most things American these fishing lures were bigger and shinier than anything the reviews editor had seen before. Monstrous they may be, he thought to himself, but I will try them out. At lunchtime on the day the box of lures arrived he set off for the Thames where it runs through the Home

Park. Here the fishing was still at that time free, but our intrepid editor – though known to be eccentric to the point of lunacy – was well aware that using these giant lures he had not the slightest chance of catching anything. No. The real purpose of this visit to the river was just to see if he could cast the damned things! He took with him a powerful salmon spinning rod and a big multiplier reel packed with 20-pound nylon. When he reached the river he decided to fish just below the railway bridge where the water was very fast and very deep.

He took a three-jointed eel plug. It was wooden, heavily weighted with lead and at least 8in (20.3cm) long. Mumbling about Americans always trying to make everything larger than it needed to be he tied on the massive lure – which looked vaguely like an eel – and hurled it out into the middle of the river. It hit the water, sank and began to swing round in the current. The pressure of water on the line and the sheer weight of the lure made it feel as if a pretty hefty fish was already attached to the line. 'What on earth can this thing have been designed to catch?' wondered the reviews editor as the lure rose from the depths and he prepared to cast it out again.

The lunch hour wore on and the reviews editor was enjoying the rhythm of cast, wait and slowly reel in. It was time for a final throw and then back to the office. The giant eel plug sailed out over the river and landed with a final splash. It began to sink and the current took it round. The reviews editor started to reel in. Seconds later there was a massive thump and the powerful rod was almost pulled out of his hands. The clutch on the reel had been screwed right down, but as the rod bucked and kicked line was disappearing rapidly from the drum. The reviews editor assumed he was fast asleep and this was all a dream. There were no large fish in the Thames and even a big barbel – a really big barbel – would hardly be able to do this to a salmon spinning rod and 20-pound breaking strain line.

After two or three massively powerful runs the fish – if indeed it was a fish – showed signs of tiring and ten minutes later the reviews editor peered carefully down into the water where his line disappeared, expecting any moment to catch his first glimpse of a shark or conger eel.

At last he saw it – an absolutely beautiful brown trout that must have weighed at least 6lb (2.7kg), but hooked neatly through the top of the tail fin. It must have seen the eel lure as it swept round in the current and, outraged by this intruder, gave it a whack with its tail. But that whack nearly cost the trout its life. Luckily for the trout this was the close season and the reviews editor was a stickler for seasons and fair fishing. The trout was foul hooked and had to go back. It had seemed like a 40lb (18.1kg) salmon precisely because, being hooked in the tail, it could fight ten times as hard as it would normally.

Thames trout in Victorian times had been famous for their size, their beauty and their fighting prowess, but they were believed to be virtually extinct at the time this incident took place. The reviews editor was astonished and delighted. He is still alive today and is probably the only man in Britain to have caught a really big wild Thames trout in modern times.

SERIAL KILLERS
ENGLAND, 1984

Pike are the ultimate freshwater killers. Anything that moves through the water is liable to arouse the pike's attacking instincts and pike are capable of terrifying turns of speed. However, there is a little-known and very different aspect to the life of the pike that only prey fish understand. Pike have often been observed surrounded by roach and dace that seem totally unafraid. Given that roach and dace are normally among the pike's favourite foods it seems odd that they don't always give this fearsome predator a wide berth. The reason is probably that some kind of electrical change in the water tells the roach and dace that this particular pike is not in feeding mode. When a pike is in feeding mode it will look pretty much as it would always look to a fisherman observing the goings-on beneath the water through a pair of binoculars, but at times like this not a prey fish will be seen anywhere within range.

The odd behaviour of the pike has produced some remarkable catches. On one occasion on a wide Norfolk broad a fisherman spinning for pike hooked a fish of 1lb (0.45kg). This pike – or jack as it should be called – was promptly knocked on the head, put on a very large hook and cast out in hopes of a much mightier fish. An hour passed and a sudden run almost yanked the fisherman's rod into the mere. He caught it just as it disappeared over the side of the boat and five minutes later landed a 2lb (0.9kg) jack.

The second fish hadn't even been hooked. It had sunk its teeth into the smaller pike's head and been unable to let go.

The fisherman was not amused. He was used to catching pike of 20–30lb (9.1–13.6kg) and he had chosen this particular water because it had a reputation for producing big fish, but this was clearly one of those days when the pike – all the pike, whatever their size – were feeding.

On a whim the fisherman knocked this second pike on the head and attached it to his biggest hook and his strongest tackle. The bait was so big he couldn't cast it out. Instead he dropped it over the side of the boat and then rowed over to a dense reed bed towing the 2lb pike behind. When he reached the reed bed he stopped towing the pike. He left it at the edge of the reeds and rowed back to the middle of the lake, paying out line all the time. No sooner had he settled down to wait than his big old centre-pin reel began to turn faster and faster. He mumbled, 'Tell that to the marines!' under his breath and struck. Immediately he knew that this was no ordinary fish. With its first run it managed to take out more than 80 yards (73.2m) of line and then it did a thing that few really big pike do – it jumped clear out of the water before settling back for a long, dogged fight. It took nearly half an hour to subdue that pike but it was the biggest fish ever taken from that particular lake. It weighed a little under 40lb (18.1kg) and is the only recorded instance of a pike taking a pike that had taken a pike.

ESCAPE AT LAST

SCOTLAND, 1986

The British record salmon of 64lb (29kg), which was caught in the 1920s and also happens to be the biggest fish of any species ever caught in fresh water in Britain, was hooked and landed by a young woman and it has often been said that if women spent more time fishing they would very likely do far better at it, generally speaking, than men. Big fish present special difficulties and it may be that what women are said to lack in physical strength, compared to a man, they more than make up for in intelligence and with a very big fish intelligence is absolutely vital if you are to have any chance of success. The sad thing about large fish, too, is that as high-seas netting for salmon increased in the 1970s and 1980s, salmon stocks plummeted and big fish reaching the rivers became very rare indeed. But it does still happen and it happened to a man fishing the Beauly in Scotland in 1986.

The fisherman was enormously experienced and he had caught 40lb (18.1kg) salmon before. He was fishing on a day when conditions for the fly seemed absolutely perfect and on his very first cast he felt a savage pull. Judging by the enormous strength of the fish's first run the fisherman was convinced it was a specimen well over 30lb (13.6kg).

That first bid for escape was so powerful that the fisherman had to run along the bank just to stay in touch. The fish ran on and then the fisherman found his path blocked by a series of huge rocks. He looked down and watched his backing line – nearly 100 yards (91.4m) of it – gradually disappear. Within seconds the drum was visible beneath what little backing remained and the line parted. The fish had gone. But when the gillie came up he suggested they go in search of the rest of the backing – the 80 yards (73.2m) or so left adrift, but probably no longer attached to the fish. They took a boat and tried every part of the pool and just as they were about to give up they saw the line apparently stationary and over against the far bank. The fisherman tied a big fly to what little backing remained on his reel and with incredible good luck he managed to snag the trailing line first time. He retied the lost backing to the few yards of line remaining on his reel and began to reel in. Astonishingly the fish was still at the other end.

Hour after hour passed with the massive fish moving up and down the pool. It could not be drawn into shallow water, nor out of the main current into an area of deeper slack water. Then, with a massive display of power the fish bolted for a pool further down the river and there was nothing the fisherman could do but throw his rod into the water and hope to fish it out again further downstream.

With the help of his gillie and some skilful manoeuvring in the boat they found the rod, but the line had broken again. The fisherman, who must have been exhausted by this time, decided that they should accept defeat. The gillie, loath to give up, persuaded him to look once again for the broken line. It must have seemed almost unreal when once again they spotted the end of the line drifting in the lower pool. With the end of the line re-attached to the reel line the battle began once again. The real size of this extraordinary fish can best perhaps be judged by the fact that after several hours it still showed no signs of tiredness. An hour or so later the rod had once again to be thrown into the water and chased by boat. This time the line didn't break and it began almost to seem that against all the odds this fish might be landed. Twice they had seen the fish – it was probably a little less than 4ft (1.2m) long, but of unusual depth. He jumped just once and the splash must have been like a sack of coal hitting the water.

Almost eight hours after he'd been hooked and just as the fisherman was easing him up towards the net the fly pulled out of his jaws and he was gone – this time for good. Estimates of fish weight are always difficult but given that the fisherman had successfully played 40-pounders (18.1kg) in the past it seems that this rare giant that had somehow evaded the nets and the seals may well have weighed 50lb (22.7kg) or more.

A VERY ODD BAG

WYLAM, NORTHUMBERLAND, 1989

A boy fishing the tidal River Tyne at Wylam a few miles inland from Newcastle upon Tyne was astonished when he caught a flounder – a sea fish. Wylam is after all more than 20 miles (32.2km) from the sea. Then imagine his surprise when minutes later he caught a brown trout in precisely the same spot.

He wondered what surprises the river might still have in store for him as he cast his fly line once more. Back and forth it went as he gradually increased the length of the line to reach the middle of the river. But he misjudged his timing and the line fell into the field behind him. Then, as he reeled in ready to start again, imagine his amazement when he hooked a rabbit that had been quietly nibbling the grass. He let the rabbit go as it seemed rather unsporting to keep it after hooking it like a fish. Then, as the light failed and he began to consider going home, he finished a remarkable day by catching a fresh-run, 10lb (4.5kg) salmon.

POT OF GOLD

ENGLAND, 2007

From the mid-1850s until the 1980s much of the lower River Thames was not worth fishing – it was simply too polluted.

But the gradual departure of most of London's factories, power stations and dirtier industries, not to mention a remarkable clean-up campaign that saw sewage moved downstream to the estuary by pipe, led to an astonishing transformation.

Fishermen began to notice that at Hammersmith and Putney, at Fulham and Chelsea, you could once again see the golden gravel beneath the flowing water. Centuries of pollution were being swept away and though they were sometimes laughed at by their friends, fishermen began once again to ply their rods along the lower river, even down as far as the House of Commons and the Tower of London.

Astonishingly, even fly fishermen began to seek the legendary Thames trout – and trout are always among the last species to return to a once-polluted river. Then, in 2005, the fishing world was astounded when reports came in that a 2½lb (5.5kg) trout had been caught by a fly fisherman fishing, of all places, next to a refuse lorry depot at Wandsworth.

But the strangest story of all from this re-birth of the river came in 2007 when a clockmaker from Isleworth took his grandson fishing just below Kew Bridge.

Legering with heavy weights and bunches of small worms

they had caught several bream and a good-sized perch and were about to pack up and go home when the grandson hooked something heavy just below one of the stone piers of the bridge. It didn't fight like a fish and at first he assumed he'd simply snagged a rock but gradually the heavy weight came in. It turned out to be a canvas bag which clanked very oddly as they unhooked it. When they cut it open the bag contained more than a hundred coins from the Victorian period and earlier, including numerous silver sixpences.

Not to be outdone, on their next outing the grandfather hooked a zander and a trout on two consecutive casts, a feat impossible to imagine a generation earlier.

OTTER'S BREAKFAST

ENGLAND, 2013

Night fishing has grown hugely in popularity as tents – or bivvies as they are known among fishermen – have become lighter and more comfortable, and tackle and torches have improved beyond all recognition. What used to be a cold, arduous activity has become comfortable and exciting at the same time, for there is no doubt that bigger fish are often more likely to be caught at night when rivers and lakes are quiet, boat traffic has gone and calm descends.

But there can be something extremely eerie about fishing at night – the wind makes strange noises in the trees, and animals and birds unheard and unseen during the day emerge to hunt and forage.

Many night fishermen have looked down to see a hedgehog upended in their tin of worms busily gorging on what it sees as a free meal. And foxes often make their presence felt, their eyes caught for an instant in the glare of a flashlight.

An angler who fished regularly on the River Windrush in Oxfordshire had a strange experience one night while fishing for barbel. It was a moonlit night in June with hardly a breath of wind and for the first few hours nothing stirred and only the sound of the river could be heard.

Then, without warning, he felt a tremble on the line he held gently in his left hand. There was a tug and the line began to slip through his fingers. He lifted the rod quickly but it was too late – whatever had taken his bait was now gone.

Cursing, he decided he would use one of his electronic bite alarms. He hated them and much preferred touch legering but he needed some sleep and the buzzer alarm would be loud enough to wake him if a barbel took his bait.

Having adjusted his tackle, he lay down half in and half out of his little tent and soon fell asleep. It was almost morning when he woke. He lifted his head, still half asleep, and peered down past his feet and out through the front opening of the tent.

There, not 2ft (61cm) from his outstretched legs, was an otter busily chewing the front end of a large brown trout. Even when he shifted his position and propped himself up on his elbows the otter continued calmly to eat its breakfast. A minute or two later the otter quietly trotted off along the bank.

That would have been astonishing enough on its own, but the very next night, just as dawn broke, the very same thing happened again – the same otter arrived at his tent and proceeded to eat its breakfast.